THE HOME STRETCH

THE HOME STRETCH

Dale Evans Rogers

with Floyd Thatcher

WORD BOOKS
PUBLISHER
WACO, TEXAS

IN CANADA: G. R. WELCH
BURLINGTON, ONTARIO

Unless otherwise indicated, Scripture quotations are from the King
James Version of the Bible. Other Scripture quotations are from the
following sources:

The New Testament in the Language of Today (Beck) by William F. Beck.
Copyright © 1963 by Concordia Publishing House.
The Bible: An American Translation (AAT) by J. M. Powis Smith and Edgar
Goodspeed. Copyright © 1935 by the University of Chicago.
The Jerusalem Bible (JB), copyright © 1966 by Darton, Longman & Todd,
Ltd. and Doubleday and Company, Inc. Used by permission of the
publisher.
A New Translation of the Bible (Moffatt) by James Moffatt. Copyright ©
1954 by James Moffatt.
The New American Standard Bible (NASB), © The Lockman Foundation
1960, 1962, 1963, 1968, 1971, 1972, 1973, 1975, 1977.
The New English Bible (NEB), © the Delegates of The Oxford University
Press and the Syndics of The Cambridge University Press, 1961, 1970.
Reprinted by permission.
The New International Version of the Bible (NIV), copyright © 1978 by
the New York International Bible Society. Used by permission of
Zondervan Bible Publishers.
The New King James Version (NKJV). Copyright © 1979, 1980, 1982,
Thomas Nelson, Inc., Publishers.
The New Testament in Modern English (Phillips) by J. B. Phillips, published
by the Macmillan Company, © 1958, 1960, 1972 by J. B. Phillips.
The Four Gospels (Rieu) translated by E. V. Rieu. Copyright © 1953 by
Penguin Press, Ltd.
The Revised Standard Version of the Bible (RSV), copyrighted 1946, 1952,
© 1971, 1973 by the Division of Christian Education of the National
Council of the Churches of Christ in the U.S.A., and used by permission.
Today's English Version of the Bible (TEV), copyright © American Bible
Society 1966, 1971, 1976. Used by permission.

Library of Congress Cataloging in Publication Data:

ISBN 0-8499-0344-0

Printed in the United States of America

67898 BKC 987654321

Contents

The Home Stretch

Have you ever wondered why some people seem old at forty while others are young at seventy? I have. And as I've thought about it, I have come to believe that the secret is found in a rather obscure Old Testament verse. In a completely different setting and under circumstances we have difficulty imagining, the people of Israel heard these words from Moses' lips in one of his final speeches before his death, "I have set before you life and death, . . . therefore choose life" (Deut. 30:19, RSV).

"The straight part of a race track from the last turn to the finish line."

The dictionary definition of *the home stretch* has a rather sterile and lifeless sound. But if you are sitting in the middle of an expectant crowd in the stands at a race track when a field of horses rounds that last turn, excitement reaches a fever pitch as their strides lengthen for the dash to the finish line. These are electric moments! Rider and horse appear molded together as one, both straining forward and giving it all they've got in anticipation of those last yards.

The Home Stretch

A Time to "Strain Ahead"

It is this mood and excitement that caused the apostle Paul to come alive when he wrote to his friends in Philippi, "I have not yet won, but I am still running, trying to capture the prize for which Christ Jesus captured me. I can assure you my brothers, I am far from thinking that I have already won. All I can say is that I forget the past and *I strain ahead for what is still to come;* I am racing for the finish" (Phil. 3:12–14, JB, italics mine).

Since Paul was writing from Rome, he knew his vivid imagery of a race would appeal to his Greek readers in the Roman colony of Philippi. Depending on the reader, one of two scenes would certainly come to mind when they read Paul's words: a runner lengthening his pace for the final sprint down the straightaway or a chariot driver straining forward with death-defying intensity as he grips the reins of his plunging horses—a scene straight out of the movie *Ben Hur.*

A Time for Renewal

The imagery Paul used here and in various other places in his letters has always appealed to me. I've often been accused of living life as if it were a race. B.C.—before Christ in my life—I moved down the fast track in my drive for fame and what I thought

then was success in show business. And then on that
Sunday evening so long ago, when Dr. Jack
MacArthur gave the invitation to accept the Lord, I
raced down the aisle of that First Baptist Church
of Eagle Rock and found peace and joy in the prayer
room as I came clean with God and turned my life
over to him.

My mother used to say, "Frances [my real name]
always rushes into things. She is so impulsive!" I
suppose she was right—especially since the day I
committed my life to the Lord. But life is so full
and the excitement of being a Christian is so great
that pulling out all the stops and going full speed
just comes naturally for me. This is why it is easy
for me to identify with the race image that is so
often applied to life and that Paul referred to in his
letter to the Philippians.

For several years now, I have wanted to reflect
on and write about that part of our lives we might
call the home stretch. None of us knows just how
long that home stretch will be after we've made it
into and through what we now call midlife—a
chronological range between age forty and the early
sixties. Except for living wisely and carefully, there
may not be much we can do about the length of
the home stretch, but we can exercise a great deal
of control over its quality.

And now that I can claim the distinction of being
on the other side of the traditional three score and
ten, I believe I've earned the right to have some

opinions about the home stretch, although—Lord willing—I'm still a long way from the finish line.

Of one thing you can be sure: we're not going on a nostalgia binge. I refuse to sound like a senior citizen or an "older" person or someone in the "golden years." To me, those terms and the others that are in vogue have a negative, "over-the-hill" sound. I suppose "late adulthood," used by psychologist and social scientist Daniel Levenson, is the least objectionable to me.

At any rate, I identify with Bernard Baruch, a statesman and financier who died at the age of ninety-five, when he said, "To me, old age is always fifteen years older than I am." And I would add to that, "A person's true age is to be found in the years ahead, not in those already passed."

An Adventure of Faith

But all of us, whether we're in our twenties, our forties, our sixties, or our seventies, are moving steadily toward the straight part of life's track that leads to the finish line. Each and every stage of life is part of the race. And for us Christians, it is terribly important that every inch of the straightaways and turns be a living adventure of faith irrespective of our immediate surroundings or circumstances.

The Home Stretch

A Time for Excitement and Victory

When the apostle Paul wrote that he was straining for what was still to come and that he was racing for the finish, he was apparently in prison in Rome. He was most likely still suffering from an irritating disability described earlier as a "thorn in the flesh." Undoubtedly, the ravages of four shipwrecks, thousands of miles of rugged overland travel on foot, and physical beatings had left deep physical and emotional scars. And while we don't know for sure, Paul was in all probability between fifty and fifty-five years of age—still midlife by our standards today but late adulthood in the first century.

Yet there's no sound of pessimism in Paul's writing, and he certainly isn't complaining about "getting old." Quite the opposite—he's straining ahead and looking forward eagerly. We get a picture of a man who is alive every minute, enjoying the present and anticipating the future.

In a keynote commencement address at Pepperdine University in Malibu, California, Norman Cousins (former editor of *Saturday Review* and author of *Anatomy of an Illness*) made this incisive comment to the graduating students in the Graduate School of Education and Psychology: "The great tragedy of life is not death but what dies inside of us while we live."

He is so right! But then I'd add, "The great tragedy

of life is that so many Christians, instead of going into a sprint on the home stretch, seem to lose their zest for life and begin to coast. They look back instead of ahead and begin to sound like 'old folks.'"

Eternal Life Has Already Begun

For the Christian, eternal life has already begun. And I believe that, short of an unexplainable debilitating illness, God intends for us to be full of life and busy for him.

I like the way the *Jerusalem Bible* speaks of Abraham's death: "The number of years Abraham lived was a hundred and seventy-five. Then Abraham breathed his last, dying at a ripe old age, an old man who *had lived his full span of years*" (Gen. 25:7–8, italics mine). I have the same feeling about Abraham that I have about the apostle Paul—he was always straining ahead and racing for the finish. In my dreams, I've had mental pictures of both Abraham and Paul. I've imagined them in all sorts of situations. But I've never visualized them relaxing in a rocking chair.

Moses, an Old Testament Model

Have you ever wondered why some people seem old at forty while others are young at seventy? I have.

The Home Stretch

And as I've thought about it, I have come to believe that the secret is found in a rather obscure Old Testament verse. In a completely different setting and under circumstances we have difficulty imagining, the people of Israel heard these words from Moses' lips in one of his final speeches to them before his death: "I have set before you life and death, . . . therefore *choose* life" (Deut. 30:19, RSV, italics mine).

Moses seems to be telling them that the choice for *life* was theirs. They could decide whether or not to live—to be really *alive.* And I believe Moses knew what he was talking about. He was older than most of us who are reading this book when he led more than a million of his fellow Hebrews out of Egypt into the unknown of the Sinai Peninsula. Moses had *chosen* to live. And he had gone on for forty more years to live a vigorous life under the most difficult of circumstances. In fact, the writer of Deuteronomy wrote this epitaph, "Moses was a hundred and twenty years old when he died; his eye was not dim, nor his natural force abated" (34:7, RSV). This is why Moses is one of my real-life heroes.

From Socrates to Bob Hope

From Moses, my mind wanders down through the years to others who stand out because of their accomplishments on the home stretch. Socrates learned to play a musical instrument in his old age.

15

The Home Stretch

Cato, the Roman soldier, statesman, and writer, learned Greek when he was eighty.

Michelangelo did some of his finest work as an artist when he was ninety. Verdi composed *Ave Maria* when he was eighty-five. Tennyson wrote "Crossing the Bar" when he was eighty, and comedian George Burns won an Oscar when he was eighty. Then there's Mother Teresa and Bob Hope, who have accomplished so much on the home stretch.

Two Special Examples

But two names especially stand tall in my mind. First, there is the prize-winning author, James Michener, who wrote *Hawaii, The Source, Texas,* and many other bestsellers. Several years ago, at the age of seventy-five, he said, "I can hardly wait to get out of bed in the morning. I have so many exciting things I want to do." Mr. Michener has chosen life, and it is obvious that he has deliberately set out to live his full span of years.

The other person who stands tall in my life and memory is Mrs. Charles E. Cowman, who with her husband was a pioneer missionary to Japan and China in the early 1900s. In 1917, because of Mr. Cowman's ill health, they returned to the United States, where he died.

In 1925, at the age of fifty-five, Mrs. Cowman's first book, *Streams in the Desert,* was published and has now sold well over two million copies. Then, at age seventy-nine, she published a daily devotional book for young people entitled *Mountain Trailways for Youth*. When she was eighty-two, her *Traveling Toward Sunrise* was published and became a top seller in the devotional marketplace. Mrs. Cowman awakened a new person every morning, and she epitomized the words she had written earlier in life, "Unlike the flesh, the spirit does not decay with the years. We can keep on living abundantly and creatively until we die, no matter at what age."

This great Christian, whose words have touched millions of lives, died at the age of ninety. There was a parallel between her life and a story she once told: "Somewhere near the snowy summit of the Alps there is an inscription that marks the last resting place of an Alpine guide. Just three short words tell the story, 'He died climbing.' We often hear it said that a certain person is 'growing old.' But we don't grow old. We only *get* old when we cease to grow and climb."

Living with an Expectant View of the Future

There seems to be a common cord that binds together the experiences and stories of all of these people I've just mentioned. They lived life with an expectant view of the future. From their point of view, they were never finished. There had to be a tomorrow because there were so many exciting things they wanted to do.

This idea was well expressed by Dr. Viktor Frankl, psychiatrist and survivor of a World War II Nazi concentration camp. Throughout his prison experience, he observed the reactions of his fellow sufferers, and somewhere he made this comment: "Survivors were people who believed they were unfinished with life." And in one of his important books, he built on this idea when he wrote, "It is a peculiarity of man that he can only live by looking into the future."[1]

Somewhere I picked up this little poem. I'm not sure who wrote it, but it ties in perfectly with what Dr. Frankl has written:

> Age is a quality of mind—
> If you have left your dreams behind,
> If hope is lost,
> If you no longer look ahead,
> If your ambitions' fires are dead—
>   Then you are old.

We Choose Our Future

For me, the picture is beginning to come into focus. Late adulthood—the home stretch—is nothing more than the extension of a race that started with that first smack on the bottom and the first cry. Each day, each week, each year, and each decade build toward the home stretch. And what we are then is the result of the attitudes and dreams and hopes that we hugged to ourselves during our younger days. Dr. Paul Tournier, that much-beloved Christian psychiatrist from Geneva, understood this so well when he wrote, "In order to make a success of old age, one must begin it earlier."[2] In other words, our success in the home stretch is determined by the way we lived during our twenties, our forties, and our sixties.

At each stage of life, *we choose* what the next will be like. We decide whether tomorrow is flooded with sunshine or beclouded with oppressive storms, whether to change and grow or to remain static and get stale. It is *our* decision to be optimistic, to dream, to have hope, to live on tiptoe.

But even as I write these words, I want you to know that, of course, God's ways are not our ways. No matter how we choose or dream or hope, we will experience wrenching hard times, intense disappointments, and the ravages of grief. But even then, we choose our method and style of coping.

No, I'm not a Pollyanna thinker. But I have come to learn that our wonderful heavenly Father created us in his image. And as his redeemed sons and daughters, we possess the capability to think and act and live so that *every* part of our race is well run, especially that most exciting and potentially productive part of all—the home stretch.

The Home Stretch

Grow a Little Each Year

Few writers have blessed the American scene more
than nineteenth-century poet Henry Wadsworth
Longfellow, who gave us such masterful works as
Evangeline, The Song of Hiawatha, and *Tales of a
Wayside Inn.* In the midst of all of his successes,
though, were two great sorrows—First, the ill-timed
death of his young wife in Holland and then, years
later, the loss of his second wife, who was fatally
burned in an accident at home.

Apparently, not long before Longfellow's death at
age seventy-five, an admirer asked him how he
continued to write so beautifully and remain so
vigorous. Longfellow responded by pointing to an
apple tree that was a riot of colorful bloom and said,
"That is a very old apple tree, but the blossoms this
year seem more beautiful than ever before. That old
tree grows a little new wood each year, and I suppose
it is out of the new wood that these blossoms come.
*Like the apple tree, I try to grow a little new wood
each year.*"

I believe Mr. Longfellow had discovered a very
simple yet profound truth. Life comes out of "new
wood"—new growth. But the analogy shifts a bit
when we move from apple trees to people. God,
through the awesome and magnificent forces of
nature, acts to produce "new wood" in the apple
tree. But growth in the human realm is a deliberate
choice of people. We *decide* to keep growing

throughout our lives. When that decision is made, there are certain specific things we can do to enhance that growth process. And God has built into us the capability of doing those things that can and will contribute to our success in the home stretch.

But age is not a factor. Maggie Kuhn of the Gray Panthers understood this when she said, "Old age is not chronology. It's self-image and state of mind."

Maggie Kuhn's view of age was certainly shared by Mr. Hokusai, a talented Japanese artist, who at age seventy-five wrote, "From the age of six, I had a mania for drawing. . . . By the time I was fifty, I had published an infinity of designs; but all I produced before seventy is not worth taking into account. At seventy-three I learned a little about the real structure of nature, of animals, plants, birds, fishes. In consequence, when I am eighty, I shall have made still more progress; at ninety I shall penetrate the mystery of things; when I am one hundred, I shall certainly have reached a marvelous stage; and when I am one hundred and ten, everything I do, be it but a dot, will be alive."[3]

Physical energy may indeed diminish on the home stretch, but the Lord has given us another energy that is far more important and effective. It is this that we want to look at in the rest of our visit together.

The Energizing Power of a Positive Attitude

We aren't "grasshoppers" in a world piled high with giant difficulties. But if we allow our minds to become polluted by negative attitudes—if we think defeat—we lose sight of our possibilities in Jesus Christ.

One of the most powerful sources of energy the good Lord has blessed us with does not come in a medicine bottle and cannot be administered with a shot. In terms of dollars and cents, it isn't expensive, yet it is a vital ingredient of life at every stage—especially as we move toward the home stretch. This great energy source has more than once changed the course of history, as both leaders and ordinary people have asserted *a positive attitude.*

There are those in some circles today who label this idea as superficial or phony. But I don't believe that for a minute. In fact, I've discovered that only a tough-minded person has what it takes to develop and maintain a healthy and inspiring positive attitude. Then, too, I've known some folks who seem to have the ridiculous idea that a positive attitude toward this life isn't realistic, that anyone who can see the least bit of good in what's going on in our world has his or her head buried in the sand. But nothing could be further from the truth!

Who Is in Charge?

So often, we look at life through smeared glasses and allow our thoughts to be gloomy and negative. We act as if Satan was in charge instead of God— concentrating on the problems and the evil in the world instead of on the possibilities and the good. Like Peter, who was invited by the Lord one night to join him in a stroll on the waters of the Sea of Galilee, we take our eyes off of Jesus, look at the waves beating against our feet and legs, and begin to sink because our thoughts are negative and filled with fear.

Unfortunately, this sort of thing has been going on since the earliest days of our religious history. There is a fascinating story in the thirteenth chapter of Numbers that illustrates so graphically our tendency toward negative attitudes.

"Grasshopper" Attitudes

First, though, we need to set the stage for the story. The time is roughly 1300 B.C., and the setting is Egypt, where the Hebrew people have been in slavery for about four hundred years. The characters are Moses and the Egyptian pharaoh.

Moses had been separated from his countrymen in Egypt for many years, but now he was back after his dramatic meeting with God at the burning bush near Mount Sinai. It was there Moses had received his commission to return to Egypt as God's messenger to the king, and it was there he had been told that he would lead his people to freedom.

The story of the spiritual tug-of-war between Moses and the great Egyptian pharaoh (Exod. 5–12:36) is a combination of suspense and high drama. Interspersed in the action were the nine plagues God sent as convincers that the Hebrews should be released. But the impasse continued until the firstborn in every Egyptian home was struck by the angel of death. Only then did Pharaoh give them permission to leave Egypt.

About two million Hebrews made a hasty exit with Moses as their leader. But they hadn't been traveling long before Pharaoh regretted his decision and dispatched an army to round them up and bring them back.

The Hebrews by this time had reached the edge of the Red Sea. Ahead was an impassable body of water, and behind was the pursuing army of Pharaoh. It was a real Catch-22 situation, but God told Moses to stretch his arm and staff out over the water. The master storyteller of the book of Exodus left us a vivid picture: "Then Moses stretched out his hand over the sea, and all that night the Lord drove the sea back with a strong east wind and turned it into dry land. The waters were divided, and the Israelites went through the sea on dry ground, with a wall of water on their right and on their left" (Exod. 14:21–22, NIV).

The second act of that drama was played out with the Egyptian army down in the bed of the Red Sea pursuing the Israelites. When the last of the Israelites had scrambled to high ground on the other side, the Lord told Moses to stretch out his hand over the sea again. And when he did, the waters rolled back into place with a roar, and the entire Egyptian army was drowned.

We don't have a day-by-day journal of what happened after that, but we do know that God led that undisciplined and noisy mob of about two million people on into the Sinai wilderness. From there they turned north to the wilderness of Paran until they reached the area of Kadesh-barnea, some forty to fifty miles south of Beersheba on the border of Canaan.

Through all of this trip from Egypt, however long it took and by whatever route they traveled, the Hebrews had been led, provided for, and delivered by God. Imagine! From the moment they had walked on the dry bed of the Red Sea with the water stacked high on either side, God had taken care of them. And he had continued to care for them throughout every mile of the trip. They saw one "miracle" after another.

That's the setting—now for the story. God told Moses to select one man from each of the twelve tribes of Israel and send these men north to reconnoiter Canaan. Each one of the twelve were leaders and chiefs—men of responsibility. They were commissioned to scout out the country, observe the people and the fortifications, and check out the crops and food resources.

We're told they went as far north as Hebron, about twenty or so miles south of the city we know of as Jerusalem in what would someday be Judea. The twelve men scouted the area for forty days and then returned to where the Israelites were camped. They were loaded down with produce and fruit— pomegranates and figs are mentioned. The writer who described the event even said, "They lopped off a vine branch with a cluster of grapes, which two of them carried away on a pole" (Num. 13:23, JB). Imagine, the cluster of grapes was so big that it took two men to carry it!

Then, after admitting that Canaan was a land that flowed "with milk and honey," the men went on to paint a black picture of doom and gloom. They reported that the people were powerful—stronger than they were. And they said, "The country we went to reconnoiter is a country that *devours* its inhabitants. Every man we saw there was of enormous size. Yes, and *we saw giants* . . . *We felt like grasshoppers"* (Num. 13:32–33, JB, italics mine).

A Positive View

Two of the returning scouts had a positive and optimistic attitude. They urged their countrymen to march and conquer. Caleb, one of the two, said, "We are well able to do it" (Num. 13:31, JB). The other ten, though, filed the majority report, "We are not able to march against this people; they are stronger than we are" (v. 31). The majority opinion prevailed, and the feeling ran so strong against the two positive thinkers that "the entire community was talking of stoning them." It was only the intervention of the Lord that saved them from death (Num. 14:10–12, JB).

With our 20/20 hindsight vision, it is easy for us to be critical of those unbelieving and negative-thinking Israelites. And yet, over thirty-five hundred years later, our attitudes so often are much like theirs. We see ourselves as "grasshoppers" in a world of "giants." And this is true even though we have the advantage of seeing God at work throughout all intervening history, including perhaps the greatest miracle of all—the life, death, and resurrection of Jesus Christ.

As paradoxical as it may seem, the way of the Cross is the way of positive attitudes, for the Resurrection followed the Cross. It was on that first

The Energizing Power of a Positive Attitude

Easter morning that life's negatives were turned into positives; and since then, people of all times have been able to see the world through a different set of lenses.

It is God's will, I believe, for us to have a healthy, hope-filled, and positive attitude toward life, even in the troubled times that plague our world. It is true that so much of today's news is bad. We are bombarded with bad news on six o'clock television and radio. Terrorism seems to have the upper hand; brothers are killing brothers in the Middle East; the world's superpowers specialize in name calling; and the threat of a nuclear accident or war hovers over us like a black cloud. And while all of this is going on, economic patterns are shifting so that there's a restless feeling of uncertainty even in the midst of apparent growth and prosperity.

But the fact remains that we aren't "grasshoppers" in a world piled high with giant difficulties; we are the redeemed children of a good and mighty God. But if we allow our minds to become polluted by negative attitudes—if we think defeat—we lose sight of our possibilities in Jesus Christ.

No Guarantee of Utopia

Now, this isn't to suggest for a moment that I have fallen for the subtle heresy that has filtered into certain elements in the church and is creating confusion in the minds of many Christians. I'm referring to the idea that being a Christian guarantees success and prosperity—that if we have positive attitudes, give a certain percentage of our income to the church, and attend services every time the church door is open, our economic wants will be cared for and we can expect a trouble-free life.

God's grace isn't a payoff for good behavior. It isn't something we've earned or deserve. But it is ours in Christ, and it is adequate for our hard times as well as for our good times. Eugene O'Neill, in a moment of rare insight, seemed to capture this truth in a flash of inspiration when he wrote, "Man is born broken. He lives by mending. And the grace of God is the glue."

The apostle Paul knew all about this. In his letter to the Corinthian Christians, he mentioned his struggle with his "thorn in the flesh," which I mentioned in the previous chapter. He prayed three times that God would heal him. But the Lord simply answered, "My grace is sufficient" (2 Cor. 12:8–9). Then, as I read the next few verses, Paul's attitude shifted—"Most gladly therefore will I rather glory in my infirmities" (v. 9)—and he viewed his future with a positive and hopeful attitude.

The Choice Is Ours

It is a sobering thought to realize that *we choose our attitudes*. Thousands of years before the development of modern psychology, the psalmist understood the workings of our human condition when he wrote, "For as he thinks within himself, so he is" (Prov. 23:7, NASB). Or to put it another way, "We become what we think about all the time." Our attitudes are controlled by our thoughts. We decide whether to be positive people who are fun to be with or negative people whom everyone wants to avoid.

One of the most exciting ideas that has come to me is that God wants us to move into every new day with a positive attitude of hope and expectation. He wants us to *make it* at every stage of our lives, but especially during our home-stretch years. God is for us! As Christians, we are to be positive witnesses of the Good News that Jesus Christ has set us free from negatives.

What Is Our Part in the Drama?

Even though this isn't a "how to" book, I want to be very practical now. Since I believe it is God's will for us to have a positive, upbeat, and hopeful attitude toward life, and since I also believe that having positive attitudes is a deliberate choice we make, just how do we develop and expand this important gift? And it is a gift—one that God has already given us and is anxious for us to accept. But to accept that gift and put it into practice, I believe we need to accept another of God's gifts—perhaps one of the rarest. I'm referring to the gift of *knowing how to see.*

Knowing *how to see the world around us* is an important facet of this gift, for our world is perhaps one of God's strongest arguments in favor of our having a positive and hopeful outlook on life. The psalmist understood this when he wrote, "The heavens proclaim God's splendour, the sky speaks of his handiwork" (Ps. 19:1, Moffatt). And Elizabeth Barrett Browning caught a glimpse of God's creative wonder when she wrote, "Earth is crammed with heaven, and every common bush afire with God."

Earth crammed with heaven! I just don't believe it is either normal or possible for anyone to think negatively while looking out at sunrise across the high desert where we live in California, or while standing at sunset on the south rim of the Grand Canyon. It is awesome to see the wonder of God's hands at work during autumn in the Northeast, as green leaves change to a vivid splash of red and gold. And each spring in my native Texas, God's hand moves across the plains and hill country as bluebonnets and Indian paintbrush form a blue and red carpet in the open fields and along the highways.

To really *see* the wonders of God's world around us is a life-changing experience. For it is then that we participate in the divine harmony that is to be found in an intimate relationship with him.

But there's another side to the gift of knowing

how to see, a side that is a powerful force in developing positive attitudes. We must come to know *how to see ourselves as sons and daughters of God.* What an exalted place we have in God's creation! Way back in the earliest verses of the Bible, we read, "And God said, Let us make man in our image, after our likeness" (Gen 1:26). Then the sacred writer added, "So God created man in his *own* image, in the image of God created he him; male and female created he them" (v. 27).

Our Heritage in God

Those electrifying words are very specific and to the point. We are made in God's image and are in a world of his making. It is true that the entrance of sin into the world sorely disrupted God's intention for his creation. But the great Good News of our Christian faith is that the life, death, and resurrection of Jesus restored once and for all God's order for all who accept him as Lord.

I somehow suspect that Ralph Waldo Emerson, the perceptive nineteenth-century American poet and essayist, understood what this means when he wrote, "What lies behind us, and what lies before us, are small matters compared to what lies within us." And it is what lies *within* us in Christ that has the power to turn our every negative into a positive.

If we rightly claim who and what we are as

The Energizing Power of a Positive Attitude

Christians, our thoughts and attitudes are aligned with God—he is within us, and all of life becomes a positive expression of his love at work in us.

For me, one of the most awesome descriptions of what God intends us to be is found in the eighth Psalm. Evidently, the psalmist had experienced some moving moments as he looked up at the brilliance of a clear nighttime sky ablaze with stars and then reflected on his own insignificance in comparison. And then he goes on,

> Yet thou hast made him [man] little less than God,
>   and dost crown him with glory and honor.
> Thou hast given him dominion over the works of thy
>   hands;
>   *thou hast put all things under his feet.*"
>
> Ps. 8:5-6, RSV, italics mine

Imagine! God intends for us, as people made in his image, to be in charge, to exercise mastery over his creation.

How is that possible? The answer, I believe, was given us by the beloved disciple of Jesus at the very beginning of his Gospel, when he made this startling statement: "But as many as received him, *to them gave he power* to become the sons of God" (John 1:12, italics mine). In other words, as we apply this promise to our thinking here—we have the power to think and act positively at every stage of life, including every yard down the home stretch, even during those hard and difficult times.

If there ever was a person who exercised the power and ability to think and act positively during the hard times of life, it was my great hero of the faith—the apostle Paul. We take our comforts and freedom for granted as we zip down interstate highways in automobiles that do everything but steer themselves. And those of us in the Western world are so accustomed to expressing and living our faith freely that we can't even begin to imagine what it would be like to be persecuted physically because we're Christians.

But Paul gives us a pretty colorful picture as we read what his Christianity cost him:

> I realize I'm boasting recklessly, but I have worked harder, been beaten countless times, been jailed frequently, and often faced death. The Jews beat me five times within one lash of the forty-lash limit. Three times I was beaten with sticks, once I was stoned, three times I was shipwrecked, once I spent twenty-four hours drifting in the open sea. I have made innumerable trips and been threatened by storms, by thieves, by fellow Jews, and by non-Jews. I have been in danger in cities, in deserts, on the sea, and often from impostors. I have worked at the task when I was exhausted, in great hardship, during sleepless nights, without food, exposed to the cold without enough clothing.[1]

The Energizing Power of a Positive Attitude

Now, that is what I would call a vivid description of trouble and hard times. But right in the middle of that kind of life, Paul gave us one of the most earth-shaking promises in all of the Bible: "I can do all things through Christ which strengtheneth me" (Phil. 4:13). Another translation words it this way: "I can do everything through him who gives me strength" (NIV).

Even though Paul wrote those words while he was in prison, probably in Rome, he doesn't sound like a victim or like someone whose attitude has gone sour. He was a positive thinker even in jail because he knew who and what he was in Christ.

To Be a Chicken or an Eagle

Recently, while reading the little book by my friend Dr. Norman Vincent Peale entitled *You Can If You Think You Can,* I was reminded of the old story of the confused young eagle who grew up thinking he was a chicken. According to the story, a boy, whose father owned a chicken farm, was climbing to the peak of a nearby mountain one day and discovered an eagle's nest. Removing an egg from the nest, he carefully carried it down the mountain. When he got home, he put the egg into a nest with some chicken eggs that were being tended by an old hen.

Some time later, all of the eggs hatched, and the little eagle grew up with his brother and sister chicks.

For a time, everything appeared normal; the little fellow seemed to think and act like a chicken. But one day while he was out in the chicken yard pecking away at the grain, he heard a scream. And looking up, he saw an eagle soaring high above in the wind currents. Something stirred down deep inside. An unexplainable urge impelled the little eagle to spread his unused wings. Even though he had never flown before, he sensed what to do and awkwardly flew a few yards. Then, with a bit more assurance, he flew a mile or so, and from there, he soared to the mountain peak that had been his first home. He discovered who he really was and never again pecked at corn in the chicken yard.

We're Shaped by Our Thoughts

What people think is the inner force that shapes what they are and do. A hundred or so years after the apostle Paul's death, Marcus Aurelius, the Roman emperor who was also a philosopher, made this wise observation: "The soul becomes dyed with the color of its thoughts." And the wisdom writer in the Old Testament knew all about that when he wrote, "What he thinks is what he really is" (Prov. 23:7, TEV).

Happily, there are some things that don't change with the passing of time. Truth doesn't. Compare these late twentieth-century words with those of Marcus Aurelius and the Old Testament writer:

The Energizing Power of a Positive Attitude

- "One prepares for old age [the home stretch] by taking a positive attitude throughout one's life."
- "My basic rule for health, energy, and long life is to keep your thoughts healthy and positive in nature."
- "The way you think about life can influence your lifespan and your health."

These twentieth-century writers and thinkers are right in tune with the rhythm of the past.

The Home-Stretch Adventure

The home stretch of our lives is intended to be satisfying, rich, and productive. Above all, it is a time that calls for flexibility and an openness to change. But even beyond that, it is meant, I believe, to be the time of our greatest influence for good and for God. Contrary to what frequently happens, late adulthood is not a time for looking back, for living in the past. It isn't a time for grousing about the so-called "good old days." Instead, it is a time to approach each new day with excitement and anticipation.

Many years ago, noted American thinker and writer William James said, "Believe that life is worth living, and your belief will help create the fact." For the Christian, life is not only worth living; it is worth living to the fullest—positively and with exuberant optimism.

There are two great affirmations that are life changing. If daily we will fill these wonderful minds God has given us with these words, our attitudes and lives in every stage—but especially in our home-stretch years—will be filled with hope and meaning. Repeat them in the morning on awakening, in a moment of quiet at noon, and just before drifting off to sleep at night:

> This is the day the LORD has made;
> let us rejoice and be glad in it.
> Ps. 118:24, NIV

> But this I call to mind,
> and I have hope:
> That the gracious deeds of the Lord
> never cease,
> his compassion never fails;
> They are fresh every morning;
> great is his faithfulness.
> Lam. 3:21–23, AAT

Enthusiasm—
The Art of
Being Alive

I believe that anyone who has the overflowing life of Christ in them is enthusiastic and really enjoys life! And when we enjoy life, it shows—it moves out with a powerful energy that those around us can feel. It is attractive and winsome. We get a lift when we're around people that enjoy life; we're influenced by them. They make a difference in our lives.

"None are so old as those who have outlived enthusiasm." Although he died at the age of forty-four, Henry David Thoreau had learned early that enthusiasm is one of the most important ingredients of a rich, full, and useful life.

Enthusiasm—excitement about life—is important at every stage. But in the home stretch—those mature years of middle and late adulthood—enthusiasm is indispensable if we are to be the kind of people who are comfortable and at ease with ourselves. At the same time, enthusiasm is also absolutely essential if we are to be the kind of people those around us like and enjoy being with. Let's face it—limp, gloomy, and apathetic people are not especially pleasant to be around.

Enthusiasm—The Art of Being Alive

We've all had acquaintances, I'm sure, who instead of "accentuating the positive" concentrate on the negatives—the kind of folks who look at a rosebush and see the aphids or the black spot instead of the roses. It is this kind of person who instead of being awake and sensitive to the beauty of an opportunity can only see the problems.

To Be Awake Is to Be Alive

In *Walden,* Thoreau seems to relate being "awake" to that enthusiastic quality of life that he feels is important when he writes, "To be awake is to be alive." Then, a little further on, he explains what he means: "We must learn to reawaken and keep ourselves awake, not by mechanical aids, but by an infinite expectation of the dawn." I like that, for I firmly believe that as we Christians "live in expectation of the dawn," we will be awake and enthusiastic every moment of our lives—even in the midst of hard times and in our home-stretch years.

This quality of life is expressed vividly in a stirring book by Paul Horgan entitled *Lamy of Santa Fe.* With unusual flair, the author in this gripping biography describes the personhood and vitality of Juan Bautista Lamy, the first Catholic archbishop of Santa Fe.

Born in France in 1814, Lamy arrived in Cincinnati, Ohio, in 1835 as a young priest of twenty-five. Then, in 1851, he moved south and west to his "Desert Diocese"—the brawling and sprawling Southwest, consisting of northern Mexico and what is now Arizona and New Mexico. It was rugged and parched country, and only the hardiest of pioneers were able to survive. But for years, Lamy moved relentlessly across the arid and treacherous terrain of the raw frontier, ministering to the physical and spiritual needs of a people lacerated by the struggle for bare existence. His life was hard, and his experiences were often heartrending. But through it all, he maintained a spirit of high adventure that is colorfully portrayed in this descriptive comment of Horgan's: "He always awoke a young man."

What a wonderful way to express the enthusiasm, vitality, and zest for life that is meant to be ours as Christians! Being awake and alive—awaking every morning a new person—smacks of that kind of enthusiasm that energized Jesus' disciples when they finally understood that he had conquered death and the grave and was very much alive.

Actually, the drama and the miracle of that first Easter morning revolutionized all of creation. And that was seen dramatically in the changed lives of Jesus' disciples. Where three days before they had been paralyzed with fear and had gone into hiding, now they moved out into the open with seeming reckless abandon in their enthusiasm—their Spirit-intoxication. They were men *truly alive.* Fear and anxiety were forgotten; and after being empowered by the Holy Spirit at Pentecost, they moved out boldly beyond the narrow borders of Jerusalem and Judea "to the very ends of the earth" as they knew it. Theirs was a contagious faith.

Fullness of Joy—A Way of Life

Enthusiasm, a welling up of excitement, an expectation of the dawn—that is precisely what God wants for each one of us. This comes through loud and clear in so much of Scripture. The psalmist put it this way: "In thy presence is fulness of joy" (Ps. 16:11). And the words of Nehemiah are just as apropos for us now as when they were first spoken to the Jewish audience: "The joy of the Lord is your strength" (Neh. 8:10).

What a marvelous definition of enthusiasm—fullness of joy. But this joy is not the same kind of giddy, surface "happiness" that we feel when things are running smoothly and going our way. Let's face it, things don't always work out the way we plan or hope for. There's much that happens to us that hurts. But the joy both the psalmist and the author of Nehemiah wrote about is more than a feeling or an emotion. Rather, it is a way of life in which our confidence in God is so strong that we are "full of joy" even in our most difficult times.

Enthusiasm—The Art of Being Alive

An Enthusiastic Response

Moving over into the New Testament, we find a graphic picture of enthusiasm in Luke's description of the dramatic encounter between Peter and John with the crippled beggar at the Beautiful Gate of the Temple. Luke writes that after Peter had spoken the electric words, "In the name of Jesus Christ of Nazareth, *walk!*" the healed man "sprang to his feet, stood, and then walked." Then Luke continues, "He walked about, leaping and thanking God. Everyone noticed him . . . and recognised him . . . and they were all overcome with wonder and sheer astonishment" (Acts 3:7–10, Phillips).

The crippled stranger at the temple gate met two enthusiastic disciples of the risen Jesus, and he came alive with such fire and enthusiasm that everybody around got turned on. This same thing happened later when Paul and Silas began to witness for the Lord in the Greek seacoast city of Thessalonica. They hadn't been there long until it was said of them, "These men who have turned the world upside down have come here also" (Acts 17:6, RSV).

It is rather interesting to note that the word that is translated here as "turned" comes from a root word that means "to excite." Paul and Silas were enthusiastic witnesses for Christ who created excitement among their listeners. This is the authentic Christian lifestyle.

The Christian Style

Now, this kind of a mood among Christians of any age was not meant to go out of style in the first century. It is our model today whether we're bucking bumper-to-bumper traffic on Franklin D. Roosevelt Drive along the East River in New York City or on Michigan Avenue in Chicago. It is the truly Christian style in the midwestern folksiness of Muncie, Indiana, and along the seemingly endless ribbon of concrete known as Interstate 10, that winds past colorful towns in West Texas. And it is also our model on the world's longest parking lot—the San Bernardino Freeway as it converges into the interchange in downtown Los Angeles.

But so often, even among Christians, I've heard it said, "How do you expect me to be enthusiastic in a world full of bad news? I get depressed every time I read the newspapers—even the comic strips are full of tension and stress. And as for the six o'clock news on television, all we get is a depressing litany of terrorism, nuclear threats, the arms race, and name calling. I just can't see any way out of this mess, and there certainly isn't much to get excited about."

An Affair of the Will

It may not be easy—and frequently it isn't—but if a spirit of enthusiasm is the mark of an alive

Enthusiasm—The Art of Being Alive

Christian, there must be a way. And I think C. S. Lewis, with his customary perceptiveness, points the way in a comment he made about love: "Christian Love, either towards God or towards man, is an affair of the will."[1] The same principle applies equally well, I believe, to enthusiasm and being "alive": *it is indeed an affair of the will.* Nobody is enthusiastic by accident. It is something *we* decide to be and a style of life *we* decide to live.

Bruce Larson, gifted author and pastor, tells an utterly delightful story about a lady in the Seattle area who is eighty-four years old and is active in a number of worthwhile causes. She had been driving the same car for nineteen years. And evidently she had said at one time that when the old car stopped running, she would just give up and die. (It sounds to me as if she hated to buy a new car about as badly as I do.)

But one day the old engine finally belched black smoke and gave up for good. As the woman surveyed the lifeless car, though, she changed her mind and bought a secondhand, reconditioned engine. Now the nineteen-year-old car is still running—and so is she. This is what she told a *Seattle Times* reporter:

> As the cells in my body renew
> And my purpose in life I review,
> I find, growing older,
> I'm now growing bolder
> And increasingly hard to subdue.[2]

Enthusiasm—The Art of Being Alive

That lady had enthusiasm for life, and she wasn't about to quit or be subdued, even at age eighty-four!

One of the things that has puzzled me for years is the fact that so many of the Christians I meet don't seem especially enthusiastic or excited about life. As a matter of fact, it is virtually impossible much of the time to tell the difference between a Christian and a non-Christian in a busy shopping mall or department store. There's just not much "expectation of the dawn" on our faces. Somehow we flounder through the days so depressed with what might have been—loaded down with yesterday's baggage—and so filled with anxiety about tomorrow that we have no sense of enthusiasm or excitement for the present. We've gotten so busy in the scramble for existing that we have forgotten the wonder of life itself.

A "Marvelous" Encounter

Few writers have the gift of storytelling to equal Arthur Gordon. In his magnificent book, entitled *A Touch of Wonder,* he tells about getting up one morning depressed and troubled. No big crisis confronted him, but an accumulation of little things had been nibbling at his comfort zone for days on end.

The morning wore on, and things just weren't going well. When the mail came, there was nothing but window envelopes with bills in them. The day was a loser.

Needing urgently to escape the depressive atmosphere of his study, Arthur gathered up a couple of fishing rods and headed toward the seashore, where his boat was tied up: "And on the path leading down to the boat I met my friend the rabbi, walking his dogs. Or rather, my acquaintance the rabbi. We didn't know each other well. In his seventies, recently retired, he had a wonderful face, clean-shaven and strong. Pacing along with his terriers on a tandem leash, he might have been an English squire out for a stroll.

"He glanced at the two long surf rods—I always carry a spare—and then at the skiff riding offshore. 'Fishing? Alone?'

"I nodded, and spoke jokingly: 'Want to come?'

"He looked at me thoughtfully. 'Do you want company?'

"I stared at him, taken back. I was not at all sure that I wanted to share my flight with anyone. And I was quite sure that the rabbi knew as much about surf-fishing as I knew about the Talmud. Still, I *had* asked him."

A few minutes later, Arthur and the rabbi were bouncing along in the skiff on their way to the sandbar about a mile offshore. As they approached the bar, the boat took a big wave at an angle and crashed down into the trough on the other side.

Enthusiasm—The Art of Being Alive

Arthur thought his friend would be terrified, but instead the rabbi's eyes sparkled as he said, "Marvelous! Marvelous!"

They landed on the bar, and when the rabbi saw the "sculptured sand patterns" made by the waves at high tide—"Marvelous . . . The footprints of the sea." And a little later, he found a shell that still had "the sunrise in it."

When they started fishing, Arthur made the first cast for him. The rabbi tried it a couple of times, and then disaster struck as the line became a hopeless tangle from a backlash.

Arthur took the rod to see what might be done and handed the rabbi his own. Moments later a big bass struck, and the reel whined as the line raced out. Through it all the rabbi was hanging on for dear life.

The drama of the next few minutes was a comedy of errors. The rabbi stumbled and fell into the surf, and the rod flew out of his hands. Much to Arthur's amazement, when his friend recovered it, the fish was still there. The tables were turned, though; the bass was playing the fisherman rather than the other way around. Then, at the rabbi's most awkward moment, the great bass reversed its course, the leader snapped, and the fish was gone.

"The rabbi came up beside me. He was soaked, bedraggled, trembling, but there was no defeat in his eyes, no disappointment. 'Marvelous!' he said hoarsely. 'Marvelous.' " And when they parted on the shore, the rabbi thanked Arthur for "one of the great mornings of my life."[3]

The Flavor of Enthusiasm

To the seventy-year-old rabbi on the home stretch, all of life was "marvelous!" He lived "in expectation of the dawn." There is something about enthusiastic people like the rabbi that adds flavor to every stage of life—and especially during the rich home-stretch years. And since this is true, we may find it helpful to move in and take a look at some of those qualities of life that seem to be common to enthusiastic people. What kind of people are they?

(1) *Enthusiastic people usually have a wide variety of interests.* They are not one dimensional but are constantly curious and involved in different activities. Cecil Osborne, in his wonderful book, *The Art of Becoming a Whole Person,* refers to the ninety-eight-year-old retired minister who said that "his happiness in retirement was based on 'being as curious as a stray cat in a strange warehouse.' "[4]

Along with being incurably curious, a person with wide interests has a vivid sense of wonder, an insatiable desire to try new things. This is a carryover from childhood that none of us should have lost. I like to think this is at least part of what Jesus had in mind when, in responding to a question put to him by his disciples as to who is greatest in the kingdom of heaven, he said, "Hear the truth. Unless your hearts are changed and you become as little children, you will not enter the Kingdom of Heaven at all" (Matt. 18:3, Rieu).

What a marvelous comparison! The young child is always trying new things, is constantly exploring with an open mind unclouded by cynicism. Scientist Thomas Huxley understood this truth when he said, "The secret of genius is to carry the spirit of the child into old age." I think we learn from this that we are to be childlike in our interests but not childish in our attitudes. I like Cecil Osborne's observation: "Those who retain an open-eyed sense of wonder and appreciation will never grow old mentally."[5]

(2) *Enthusiastic people have a great capacity for enjoying life.* Over nineteen hundred years ago, the noted Greek biographer Plutarch observed, "For the wise man, every day is a festival." I think that is at least part of the idea behind Jesus' words: "I came so that they will have life and have it overflowing in them" (John 10:10, Beck).

I believe that anyone who has the overflowing life of Christ in them is enthusiastic and really enjoys life! And when we enjoy life, it shows—our enjoyment moves out with a powerful energy that those around us can feel. It is attractive and winsome. And we get a lift by being around other people who enjoy life; we're influenced by them. They make a difference in our lives.

Over and over again in the Gospel stories of Jesus,

we read that people followed after him. He was always surrounded by a crowd. One of the reasons for that, I think, is that he enjoyed life and was interested in all that went on around him.

Then, too, we read in Jesus' story that he was entertained at dinner parties and social events. And he evidently had a good time, even though his fellow guests weren't always those from inside temple and synagogue circles. I'm sure that Jesus' hosts were not much different than we are today—we don't invite duds and bores to our dinners or parties. Instead, we want to associate with people who are interesting, who are *alive* in every way.

I sometimes think that our Christian influence in today's world could be revolutionized for good and for God if so many of us would stop acting as if life is painful, a chore, something to be endured on our way to heaven—and looking as if we had just taken a big bite out of a lemon.

(3) *Enthusiastic people are at ease and comfortable with themselves.* They are not loaded down with the baggage of anxiety and fearfulness. I have to believe that one of the most self-assured and self-confident people in the New Testament is the apostle Paul. He was not fearful nor anxious nor insecure because he knew who he was. He exemplified these words he wrote to his Christian friends at Corinth: "For if a man is in Christ he becomes a new person altogether—the past is finished and gone, everything has become fresh and new" (2 Cor. 5:17, Phillips).

Enthusiasm—The Art of Being Alive

What a marvelous bit of good news that is! As Christians, we are becoming new persons. When we are in Christ, every day is fresh and new. In him, we have a security that enables us to be at ease and comfortable with ourselves, confident of our status as children of God. But this isn't a security that lulls us into taking it easy or playing it safe. Instead, like the eighty-four-year-old lady in Seattle, we find ourselves becoming bolder, willing to risk for God and trust him because we are secure in his love.

(4) *Enthusiastic people are effective witnesses to a life-changing faith in Jesus Christ.* Earlier I mentioned the crippled beggar at the gate of the temple. Luke wrote that after he was healed, "everyone noticed him . . . and recognised him." He was really turned on, and everybody knew it. They paid attention to him.

Have you ever noticed how easy it is to pass over or ignore a dull and listless person? Some people just fade into the background. If there is anything that turns me off, it is going into a store and being confronted by a halfhearted, negative, and insecure salesperson. I don't think any of us would be particularly impressed if we walked into an automobile salesroom and a salesman eased up and asked in a listless monotone, "You wouldn't want to buy a Buick, would you?" Buy a Buick from him? Never! I won't even go into a 7-Eleven for a jar of pickles unless the sales clerk is enthusiastic about his or her job.

Enthusiasm—The Art of Being Alive

This is why I am attracted by that healed beggar in the story. I wish Luke had told us his name. I'd like to know more about him and what happened after that memorable day.

A Present-Day Model

One of the most enthusiastic and exciting men I've ever known is Dr. Norman Vincent Peale, for many years the senior minister of historic Marble Collegiate Church in New York City. Probably more than any other living person, Dr. Peale epitomizes what it means to be enthusiastic. In one of his sermons a long time ago, he pointed out that our word *enthusiasm* is derived from two Greek words— *en* and *theos*—meaning in God or full of God. Believe me, when we understand and experience what it means to be full of God, we'll be enthusiastic!

In another one of his sermons, Dr. Peale quoted these words from *The Catholic Layman* magazine: "Every man is enthusiastic at times. One man has enthusiasm for thirty minutes—another has it for thirty days. But it is the man who has it for thirty years who makes a success in life."

This is certainly true, and at eighty-eight Dr. Peale is a living model of an enthusiastic and active lifestyle. Even as I write this, he and Mrs. Peale are planning for an extensive trip to Hong Kong and Southeast Asia. Their enthusiasm for God and for life has

Enthusiasm—The Art of Being Alive

infected people in our country and across the world
for many years.

But the great good news for you and me is that
whether we're twenty, forty, or seventy, it is never
too late to start living with the kind of attention-
getting enthusiasm that got hold of the healed
crippled man at the gate of the temple. God wants
all of us to live every day "in expectation of the
dawn" and "full of joy."

Having Friends
and Being A Friend

A friend is a person with whom we've chosen to be intimate on a deep level. Masks or defenses are not necessary, because a friend accepts us for who we are. We are accepted whether we're grumpy or out of sorts or nice to be with. There's a deep understanding that draws friends together in a healthy dependency on one another.

I firmly believe that having friends is one of our greatest gifts and being a friend is God's gift through us to someone else. Friendship is a life-changing ingredient at each turn and on every straightaway of life, but it is on the home stretch that we become increasingly aware of the richness it brings—or the loss we feel because of our earlier carelessness and indifference.

A Life-Changing Friendship

This whole idea comes alive in vivid color when I think of my friend Margie Hamilton. Let me tell you about this remarkable lady.

Having Friends and Being a Friend

The setting was our first home high up in the Hollywood hills. The time was over thirty-six years ago. Our daughter Linda Lou was playing badminton in our front yard when Margie and her severely handicapped daughter, Nancy, walked by. Without a moment's hesitation, Linda Lou called out a cheery hello and ran down to where Margie and Nancy were standing. After chatting a moment or two, Linda Lou invited them up for cookies and tea.

When I arrived home from shopping, there they all were in the living room. I recovered quickly from my surprise and joined them in a most memorable visit. It was the beginning of a long and rich friendship that was to mean more to me than I could ever have imagined at the time.

When Thanksgiving time rolled around, Roy and I invited Margie and Nancy to our home for dinner. Then by the time Robin, our "angel unaware," was born, we had become very close. God had arranged a friendship that was to help carry me through my days of agony when we realized that our little Robin was so badly handicapped. Margie, who cared for and loved her own sadly deformed Nancy, became my source of comfort during that long, dark night of the soul. It was Margie who prayed with me and loved me when I was so distraught that I couldn't pray for myself.

That life-changing friendship has enriched my life for these thirty-six years. Yes, our Robin and Margie's Nancy are now both with the Lord, but our friendship has remained close all of this time. I feel just as much at home in her postage-stamp-sized trailer house located in a desert trailer park as she does in our much larger home. Material things don't matter; what counts with each of us is God's marvelous gift of friendship for one another.

Acquaintances or Friends?

And yet one of the sad realities of our late twentieth-century culture is that while most people have acquaintances, so few have real friends. The differences are great!

Acquaintances accept us at their convenience for *what* we are. With them, our masks are always in place, our defenses are up to avoid the chance of being rejected. Acquaintances keep us on edge in our desperate struggle for acceptance and social position. By definition, they are persons we know on a casual level either socially or professionally— people we converse with superficially in the supermarket or at the office or in church or at a party. These are folks with whom we're thrown because of circumstances. We can take them or leave them without being affected much one way or another.

But it's different with a friend. A friend is a person with whom we've chosen to be intimate on a deep level. Masks or defenses are not necessary, because a friend accepts us for *who* we are. We are accepted whether we're grumpy or out of sorts or nice to be with. There's a deep understanding that draws friends together in a healthy dependency on one another.

It is this kind of a friend that is described so vividly by the writer of Ecclesiastes:

> A faithful friend is a secure shelter;
> whoever finds one has found a treasure.
> A faithful friend is beyond price;
> his worth is more than money can buy.
> Eccles. 6:14–15, NEB

It is having friends like this writer so beautifully describes and being this kind of a friend that adds richness and grace at every stage of life. But I think friendship is especially important in making the home stretch productive and fulfilling. And for the Christian, having friends and being a friend takes on special meaning as our own lives are enriched and our witness for Christ becomes more effective.

Jesus and Friends

Jesus certainly moved the word *friend* from the ordinary to the extraordinary in these words to his disciples: "This is my commandment: love one another, as I have loved you. There is no greater love than this, that a man should lay down his life

for his friends. You are my friends, if you do what
I command you. I call you servants no longer; . . .
I have called you friends" (John 15:12–15, NEB).

Since Jesus sanctified the word *friend* as he did,
and since it is friends that give our lives such shape
and meaning, it seems to me that we can all benefit
by looking closely now at what it means to be a
friend and to have friends. What are those qualities
that make a friend?

A Friend Is a Person Who Listens

I suppose if twelve different people were to
respond to that question, there would be twelve
different starting places. But the first quality I want
to mention is: *A friend is a person who listens to
us.* Active and loving listening is the greatest
compliment that we can pay to anyone.

For most of us today, listening doesn't come easy.
We're so busy "broadcasting" during our waking
hours that either we don't have time to listen or we've
forgotten how. But listening is an art we can all
acquire—*if we choose to.*

Dr. Paul Tournier, the gifted and godly Swiss
psychiatrist I've quoted so often, stressed the
importance of listening when he wrote, "It is
impossible to overemphasize the immense need
humans have to be really listened to, to be taken
seriously, to be understood. *No one can develop*

*freely in this world and find life without feeling
understood by at least one person"* (italics mine).
A friend is that one person.

Authors Floyd and Harriett Thatcher, in writing
on the importance of listening and how it is done,
explain it this way:

> Hearing is passive; listening is active. Listening
> demands concentration . . . thinking with the other
> person . . . attempting to become involved not only
> with words but with the feelings of the other person
> . . . listening with head tilted toward the speaker
> and to what is being said as well as to what isn't
> being said. In fact, listening is hard work; it requires
> energy and concentration and involvement with the
> other person. For us, listening is a meeting of the
> eyes, the windows of the soul; it is the response of
> caring; it tries hard to understand at all cost.[2]

Only a friend cares enough to listen like that.

A Friend Is Interested in What the Other Person Says and Feels

My second quality of a friend is this: *A friend is
interested in what the other person says and feels.*
Most of us are victims of perhaps the most consuming
sickness of our times—the belief that only what we
think or believe or feel matters. We are in constant

Having Friends and Being a Friend

danger of being so preoccupied in getting ahead, in doing *our* thing, in satisfying *our* own desires and needs, that we fail to express interest in the feelings and concerns of others. And yet, one of the true gains of friendship is the giving of ourselves to the interests and feelings of the people around us.

It happened many years ago—during World War II, in fact. I was sitting in the front seat of an airplane on my first U.S. Savings Bond tour as a performer. After a time, I realized that a most unattractive-looking lady had slipped into the seat beside me. Then, as I looked again, I saw that it was Eleanor Roosevelt.

In a few moments, we were deep in conversation. She wanted to know where I was going and what I would be doing. And she listened *ever* so carefully to *every* answer. I was amazed—the First Lady seemed interested in *me!* And she seemed to care about what I was thinking and about what was happening to me. Mrs. Roosevelt had the God-given gift of caring about what I said and felt. And where once I had thought she was unattractive, now she looked beautiful!

When we care enough to be interested in another person's concerns, and when we listen carefully to him or her, we make them feel good. Caring and listening builds other people up—it brings out the best in them.

It is this kind of a friend that helps us affirm our

own worth and to believe in ourselves—yes, and to love ourselves. And this is of profound importance, because linked to our capacity to love ourselves is our ability to love other people.

A Friend Can Say "I Love You"

The third quality I want to include here is: *A friend is someone who can say in words and actions, "I love you."* Somewhere I read this insightful comment by Christopher Morley: "If we discovered that we had five minutes to say all we wanted to say, every telephone booth would be occupied by people calling other people to stammer that they love them."

Too many of us, men and women alike, have what we call in my home state of Texas the "Good Ol' Boy Syndrome" (and women can have it as well as men!). A Good Ol' Boy is a Texan with a heart as big as his state. You can count on him through thick and thin no matter what, but he's tongue-tied when it comes to expressing his feelings. Now, maybe that's enough for some people. Most of us, though, need to hear the words. No affirmation says quite as much between family members or friends as "I love you."

As a rule, it is this kind of a friend, too, who has learned the importance of touching. So often, when all of the words have been said, a hug or an arm around the shoulder or a pat on the arm is the grand convincer that says, "I'm with you."

Having Friends and Being a Friend

One of the qualities of an "I love you" friend is that he or she always has time for you. I shudder to think of the number of times I may have brushed somebody off because I was in a hurry or was preoccupied with something I thought was more important. Like many people, I don't handle interruptions very well.

But then one day while reading in the Gospels, I discovered that Jesus never treated people as interruptions. It didn't matter whether he was on the road, in a boat by the lake, or in a quiet place praying, when people "interrupted" Jesus, he became present to them.

Writer Henri Nouwen tells this delightful little story about a friend of his: "A few years ago I met an old professor at the University of Notre Dame. Looking back on his long life of teaching, he said with a funny twinkle in his eyes: 'I had always been complaining that my work was constantly interrupted, until I slowly discovered that my interruptions were my work.' "[3]

The old professor had evidently made the same discovery about Jesus that I had—people were never interruptions. Jesus had time for them; and so people were healed, families were reunited, and men and women came to know God. Slowly, all too slowly, I'm beginning to understand that a friend with a need—whatever it is—must never be an interruption.

I don't know Carl Mays, but he tells a beautiful story out of his own childhood in his little book entitled *Mr. Adams: A Parable for Parents and*

Others. As a small boy, Carl became friends with Mr. Adams, a seventy-eight-year-old neighbor. It was a friendship that no one, not even his parents, seemed to understand. But as the story of their conversations moves from one incident to another, we begin to see why young Carl was attracted to his aged neighbor: Mr. Adams always listened to him; he was interested in what the boy said and thought. Mr. Adams always had time for Carl; he believed in the boy. Carl was patiently affirmed when he was right and gently corrected when he was wrong.

There was no generation gap between young Carl Mays and old Mr. Adams. Why? Because Mr. Adams had time for his little neighbor. And because of that, Carl carried beautiful memories of his old friend forward into adult life.[4]

Having time as a friend means writing a note or making a phone call to say "Thank you" or "I love you" or "You did a good job" or "I was just thinking about you and wanted you to know." Having time as a Christian friend means making a faithful commitment to pray for someone with a special need. Only God knows the strength Roy and I received from the prayers of friends during our dark hours of bereavement when we lost our children Robin and Debbie and Sandy.

The Story of Two Special Friends

There are many different stories in the Bible about outstanding friendships. Perhaps the most quoted one is about David and Jonathan. Then, of course, there's the moving story in the Gospels about Jesus' friendship with Lazarus and Mary and Martha. And while it isn't stated directly, we have to believe there were strong bonds of friendship between the twelve disciples of Jesus. There is just no way these men could have lived together as they did, day in and day out for over three years, without being close friends.

But there is one remarkable story of friendship in the New Testament that intrigues me because of the twists and turns it takes. It is the story of a Jew by the name of Joseph from the island of Cyprus and a Jew named Saul from the sophisticated university city of Tarsus in the Roman province of Cilicia.

Joseph was a Levite. And the Levites of the first century were priests involved in the administration of justice. But evidently, Joseph had become a disciple of Jesus. We first meet him early in the Book of Acts and are introduced to him by his surname, Barnabas (Acts 4:36–37).

Saul, on the other hand, was a highly educated Pharisee. Until he met the Lord in a bright light on the road to Damascus, Saul was a sworn enemy of Barnabas and of the other disciples and friends of Jesus.

It was after Saul's conversion that these two men met. We don't know exactly when they met or how, but it was most likely on Saul's first trip to Jerusalem after his conversion. It must have taken a lot of nerve for Saul to return to Jerusalem as a Christian. The last time he had been there, he had gotten warrants from the high priest that were his authority to hunt down and arrest the Christians he'd heard were active in Damascus. And it was in Jerusalem that he had been "breathing out threatenings and slaughter against the disciples of the Lord" (Acts 9:1).

But now the shoe was on the other foot. Saul was a Christian and back in Jerusalem. He wanted to share his experience with the Lord's disciples there, "but they were all afraid of him, and believed not that he was a disciple" (Acts 9:26). Saul was rejected because of his bad reputation, but Barnabas believed his conversion was real. And when Barnabas vouched for Saul, the rest of the disciples accepted him, too.

That had to be the beginning of Paul and Barnabas's friendship. It is possible they were drawn together because of a certain cultural and religious kinship. But whatever the reason was, Barnabas unselfishly stood up for his new friend. This opened the door for spiritual fellowship and for Saul to witness publicly to his new-found faith. And it was while Saul was preaching fearlessly in Jerusalem that he inspired the hatred of the Greek-speaking Jews to the point that they threatened to kill him. To save his life, Paul's Christian brethren had to whisk him out of town to Caesarea then put him on the road north to Tarsus.

Barnabas surfaced again sometime later, when the leaders in the Jerusalem church sent him to Antioch in Syria to find out what was happening among the Gentiles there who had become Christians. He was so impressed with the opportunity for Christian witness in Antioch that he traveled north to Tarsus for help. There he found the man he was looking for—Saul, whom we now know as Paul—and took him back to Antioch where they worked together in the church for a year.

From that point on, the saga of friendship unravels in high adventure. From Antioch, they made a trip back to Jerusalem. Then they returned to Antioch, where the two of them and young John Mark left on their first missionary journey. On shipboard and in traveling across the open country of southern Galatia, Paul and Barnabas worked together and ate together. They stayed together even after John Mark, Barnabas' nephew, deserted them and went home. It seemed their friendship deepened with each passing mile. The two men complemented each other; and Barnabas, sensing Paul's great ability, selflessly deferred to the leadership of his friend.

After returning to Antioch for a time, the two friends laid plans for their second missionary trip together. Barnabas expressed his desire to take John Mark with them again—he wanted to give his nephew a second chance. But Paul would have no part of that. After all, he felt, Mark had been a quitter on their last trip—and once was enough.

So sharp was the disagreement and difference of opinion between Paul and Barnabas that they separated, and we have no record that they ever traveled together again. Barnabas and Mark went off in one direction. Paul, with his new traveling companion, Silas, went in another.

Luke, as he wrote about this sad ending of a friendship, does not comment further about the separation in the Book of Acts. But we have to believe that these two sensitive and godly friends felt their separation deeply. Someone has wisely said that "to lose a friend is to die a little." I have to believe that after going through all they had together, Paul and Barnabas died a little over the breakup of their close and intimate relationship.

I also have to believe that this quarrel ultimately found the kind of healing that only the Lord can bring. It definitely appears that some years after this incident the relationship between Mark and Paul was repaired, for Paul mentions him in his closing words to the Christians in Colossae (Col. 4:10). And if Mark and Paul became friends again, it doesn't take too much imagination to believe that the rift between Paul and Barnabas was healed also.

A Friend Is Loyal

Friendship is always a risk, and Barnabas risked a great deal when he became the defender and friend of the newly converted Saul of Tarsus. From that time on, until their tragic break, Barnabas loyally boosted his friend's welfare with no apparent thought of his own position. Barnabas was exactly the kind of friend that Paul needed during those early days of his Christian experience. And while we'll not make a judgment as to who was right and who was wrong in their clash, it is not impossible that loyalty to his young nephew Mark was what caused Barnabas to stand firm in his disagreement with Paul. And most certainly, *a friend is a person who is loyal to those he or she loves.* Barnabas may have felt that Mark needed the steady hand of his friendship at that moment far more than Paul did. And it may well be it was because of the influence of his uncle Barnabas that Mark, in the years to come, was able to be a loving comforter to Paul during his last harsh prison days in Rome (2 Tim. 4:11).

"Friend" in Chinese

My friend Dr. Ted Engstrom, who for many years has been president of World Vision, has written a beautiful little book entitled *The Fine Art of Friendship.* In his introduction, he writes,

> On a recent trip to Hong Kong, I decided to do something about my gross lack of knowledge about a language now spoken by almost one-fourth of our world's people. I spent an evening with a close friend who is also a scholar of the Chinese language. In

two hours, he took me on a breathtaking whirlwind oral tour of China and its more than five thousand years of history. During the course of our visit, we discussed the Chinese word for "friend."

The current, everyday word for *"friend"* in China today is *peng yu,* but its history goes back many centuries. My tutor drew a primitive Chinese character that represented the magnificent tail of a bird called "Phoenix." This bird was so marvelous in detail that the written character came to mean something much more than "Phoenix." It slowly developed into a more generic meaning of "completeness . . . the sum total of physical beauty."

My friend proceeded to tell me that throughout the ensuing years, the literal meaning of the word was completely lost while the written character took on today's meaning of "friend, friendship, or close association."

"Why was that?" I asked.

Outer, visible beauty arrests our attention to be sure, but the true, inner beauties in people—the elegance, truth, and consistency that live within the soul of a friend—are irresistible. In friendships hearts relate to each other.[5]

The Building of Memories

It is in this relating to each other—the lasting impact of deep friendship on our lives—that multiplies its gift over and over again in the form of another of life's great gifts, the gift of memories. Somewhere author John Claypool made this penetrating observation: "A person without a memory is only half a person." If that is true, then it is equally true that a Christian with a memory is a whole person. And all of us strive with God's help and the help of our families and friends to be whole persons.

I've often wished I had been more sensitive earlier in life to building memories—memories that grow out of experiences and relationships. Close friendships may move into the distance because of a change of physical location or even death, but in our memories they remain close and alive and continue to enrich our lives.

A Gift We Choose to Accept

It is unfortunate, I think, that in the earlier stretches and turns of our lives we are often oblivious to the idea that every day we live is a time for the developing of friends and experiences that can be enriching on our home stretch. We are building memories every day that have the potential for future enrichment and meaning.

Yes, having friends and being a friend is a special kind of a gift, but as with any gift, we have to choose to accept it. And then, after accepting it, we must nurture and cultivate it in order to experience the full joy and meaning that it can bring to the home stretch of our lives.

As I've been writing this chapter, I've thought frequently about the powerful influence friends have had on my own life—how they've shaped and changed it and enriched it. At the same time, I've been painfully aware of lost opportunities for both receiving and giving friendship. Happily, though, I've also seen that my friendship book is never closed. Such being the case, I'm listing for my benefit (and, hopefully, yours) the kind of a person we need to become in order to be a friend whose "worth is more than money can buy."

To Be a Friend, We Must . . .

- *Develop and maintain an avid interest in other people.* What they think and feel is more important in the relationship than what we will get out of it.
- *Not develop relationships out of selfish motives.* We don't think of our friends as rungs up the ladder of social or professional success.
- *Learn to be active and creative listeners.* This is an art most of us will have to work at to develop. We "hear" sounds and voices, but we "listen" to people—to what they say and how they feel.
- *Have time for other people and not consider them interruptions.* An examination of our day-to-day routines might reveal that most of our time is

spent in pursuit of selfish needs and wants. I don't believe this is what the Lord had in mind when he gave us twenty-four hours a day to learn how to live.

• *Be positive and affirm other people.* Ask God to show *us* the good in others and leave everything else up to him. Practice the art of encouragement.

• *Feel free to tell our friends that we love them and appreciate them.* The kind of love Jesus said we should have for our "neighbor" is not a mere sentimental emotion. Rather, it is patient, kind, lasting—not threatened by the success of another nor cooled off by the weaknesses and failures of a friend.

Friendship Evangelism

As Christians, the Lord has called us to be his witnesses. In response to that call, evangelism has taken many shapes over the centuries. But I wonder now, in this impersonal time in which we live, if perhaps our most effective form of witnessing at every stage, but especially in the home stretch, may be *friendship evangelism.*

Creative Disciples
of Change and Growth

Living a life full of purpose calls for us to be on the move. This is not a rocking-chair-with-a-shawl-over-the-shoulders kind of existence. Rather, it holds before us at all times the adventure of change and growth, the adventure of learning and of doing new things.

"I like being seventy-five," she exclaimed, "but I will say that aging is not for sissies."[1]

That perceptive comment was part of a conversation between author Elizabeth Yates and her seventy-five-year-old friend, Dr. Margaret Henrichsen. But as I've thought about it, the aging process in all of us began on the day we were born. And I've decided that aging is not for the fainthearted at any stage of life if we grow and change and change and grow the way the Lord intends for us to do.

I remember, as I'm sure you do, the painful process of aging in the adolescent and teenage years. And then we all do a lot of aging during those fun but difficult years when our children are growing up. Some of us felt intense pain and fear on our fortieth birthday—and our fiftieth wasn't much fun either! I don't want to discourage any of you who haven't reached those last two milestones, but aging most certainly is not for timid people! And if this is true in the earlier turns and straightaways of our lives, it is especially true in the home-stretch years.

No, aging is not for sissies if we are to grow and mature and adjust to the inevitable changes that confront us as we strive to live creative and useful lives—*all* of our lives.

Coasting or Living with Purpose

But, unfortunately, so many folks slide into neutral or even reverse when they hit the home stretch. In a charming article about seventy-year-old Dr. Jonas Salk, philosopher, biologist, and developer of the first polio vaccine, writer Joan Wixen quotes the eminent scientist: "At one time, our biggest problems concerned diseases like poliomyelitis. Now we are becoming aware of another type of problem, the acute disorders of minds facing uselessness, highly developed minds suddenly without use or purpose.

"However, this doesn't have to be a problem of old age if people continue to grow as human beings and make life meaningful whether they are employed or not. Unemployment and retirement without constructive purpose are unnatural. . . . Without a constructive purpose life becomes destructive."[2]

Creative Disciples of Change and Growth

But living a life full of purpose calls for us to be on the move. This is not a rocking-chair-with-a-shawl-over-the-shoulders kind of existence. Rather, it holds before us at all times the adventure of change and growth, the adventure of learning and of doing new things.

I can't begin to tell you the number of times I've heard someone say to a retired friend, "I thought you were going to slow down and take it easy—enjoy life." But slowing down and taking it easy is the best way to grow old in a hurry. As Maggie Kuhn so wisely said, old age is not chronology. Rather it is a state of mind; it's a matter of self-image.

Taking Change in Stride

Now, I don't believe I've ever known anyone who didn't *want* to have a good self-image and a healthy state of mind. I don't believe anyone deliberately sets out to be negative. I think most of us want to grow old gracefully—to be constructively useful in every turn and straightaway of life. But living with grace and adventure and with a constructive purpose is "not for sissies" because it calls for us to become creative disciples of *change* and of *growth*.

Heraclitus, a very wise Greek philosopher who lived about five hundred years before Christ, made an astute observation for which he is famous to this day: No one can step twice into the same river, for it is always changing.

Creative Disciples of Change and Growth

And what is true of rivers is even more true of life. To resist change is to stagnate, to become uninteresting and dull. To fight change at any stage in life is to stop growing, to become gnarled and stunted. I certainly agree with writer Gail Sheehy, who wrote, "If we don't change, we don't grow. If we don't grow, we are not really living. Growth demands surrender of security. It may mean giving up familiar but limiting patterns, safe and unrewarding work, values no longer believed in, relationships that have lost their meaning."[3] But so often, in Goethe's words, "Everybody wants to be somebody; nobody wants to grow"—because growing is "not for sissies."

The Romance of the New

Somewhere I read this unidentified comment: "If you think you know all about something, you're old. And if you believe you are now doing something as well as it can be done, you are old. But if you are glad to admit that you know but little about anything, you are young."

Being open to change, to learning and doing new things, is what gives the home-stretch years a great spirit of youth and adventure. This is a time for experiencing the romance of the new, for expanding our interests and broadening our horizons. It is a time for striving to do old things better and to do new things well.

Creative Disciples of Change and Growth

A perfectly marvelous example of that can be seen in a friend of ours in Waco, Texas. Just recently, a newspaper release lauded our friend for shooting his age in eighteen holes of golf—eighty-eight. And this same friend is taking a quick course in conversational Chinese in preparation for a trip to China this year. Best of all, we didn't know he was eighty-eight until we read his golf score. We had him pegged for around seventy.

Admittedly, as we move into midlife and sort of get grooved in to doing certain things in certain ways, we tend to become set in our life patterns. We eat the same food, frequent only certain restaurants, vacation in the familiar and comfortable places where we've been before, visit with the same people, and read the same magazines and only those writers who share our particular points of view.

Learn New Things

But when we see this happening to us, it is time to set out deliberately to think and do and learn new things—possibly even things we've never done before. The sculptor Michelangelo, at ninety, having lost his eyesight, ran his hand over the statues in St. Peter's Cathedral in Rome and exclaimed, "I can still learn."

In the delightful little book entitled *How to Be Your Own Best Friend,* the authors write to this idea:

Creative Disciples of Change and Growth

"If we all just kept on doing exactly what we've done up to now, people would never change, and people are changing all of the time. That's what growth is: doing things you've never done before, sometimes things you once didn't even dream you could."[4]

A friend of ours, a delightful lady in her home-stretch years, had always attended the eleven o'clock service in her church. But one day she was told that the order and form of service was quite different at the nine o'clock hour. She thought this new experience might be interesting and exciting, so she switched; and as far as we know, she still worships at the earlier time. I like her eagerness to have new experiences even though they may involve new routines.

Then there are people we know who, in their late fifties and early sixties, have gone back to school and finished their college education or have taken graduate work. Others, like our Waco friend, have learned a new foreign language or taken a course in creative writing. Some of the most delightful children's books to be published in recent years were written by Mrs. Dorothy Hamilton, a retired Indiana school teacher. Her first book was published after she was sixty. She then went on to write over twenty more to the delight of children throughout the Midwest.

In an Associated Press release of May 1985, the writer quoted Miss Ruth Clark, age ninety-seven:

We believe in plenty of laughs and many interests,
the first of which for me was music. In my opinion,
it is the continuing interest in a variety of subjects
. . . that greatly enhances one's life, makes living a
joy and tends to smooth over the rough spots in
life that everyone must learn to endure.

Incidently, Miss Clark's other interests include
oceanography and the Boston Red Sox baseball
team.[5]

Then I read about another lady who is sixty-nine
years old and "has more unfinished projects stacked
in various places in her cluttered workroom than she
can keep up with." Her interest in learning has
evidently been lifelong and includes extensive
research and writing on the Indians of Texas.

And in our own case, it would be very easy to
settle down in the ease and comfort of our Apple
Valley home. But Roy keeps quite busy at the Roy
Rogers Museum in Victorville, and he travels some
for the Marriott Corporation, which holds the
franchises to the Roy Rogers Family Restaurants. He
is also connected with Thousand Trails, a
campground for travelers. And as I write this we
are about to break ground for the first Roy Rogers-
Dale Evans Happy Trails Resort near Phoenix. In
addition to all of this, I travel a great deal, speaking
and appearing on television. Life is an adventure
for us, even though we're both on the other side

of that three score and ten. And we'll keep it up as
long as the good Lord gives us health and strength.

The Ability to Dream and Use Imagination

Another part of the growth process that can enrich
our lives and in turn enable us to enrich the lives
of others is our ability to dream and freely use our
imagination during our midlife and home-stretch
years. So often along about that time, we have a
tendency to look back, live in the past, and yearn
for what we label the "good old days."

It is true as we said earlier that memories are
important, but only as they help us live more vibrantly
in the present and in the future. To live in the past
is a horrible waste of God's creative energy. And
besides, I'm not so sure the good old days were all
that good. I remember my childhood days in Italy,
Texas, without air conditioning and 110 degrees in
the shade—when you could find it. Those days
weren't all so good! Frankly, I think *now* is the great
time to be alive.

It is thrilling to live in the time of space exploration.
I still get goose bumps when we see pictures on
our television screens of Saturn and Uranus taken
by spacecraft and relayed millions of miles back to
earth. And to see close-up pictures of Halley's Comet
taken from a spaceship is a once-in-a-lifetime
experience, since the comet makes its appearance
only every seventy-six years or so.

Creative Disciples of Change and Growth

Yes, now is a very special time to be alive, especially as we view the present and look forward to the years ahead. Today, as never before, though, our true age lies in the lifespan ahead, not in the past.

I remember so well the lyrics to a song that was popular many years ago: "When I grow too old to dream . . ." Nonsense! I don't believe God wants us to grow too old to dream, to use our imaginations, to look expectantly into the future. The whole and very alive person plans eagerly for the future. He or she doesn't travel bumper to bumper but keeps looking far ahead down life's road with an eye toward what is just beyond the next hill or around the next turn.

I was delighted this year when my husband, Roy, planted some young fruit trees in the "back forty" of our deep lot bordering on the golf course in Apple Valley. It will probably be several years before those trees even begin to bear fruit. But Roy is always planning for the future.

Growth through Struggle

It is true, of course, that our view of the future doesn't always come from a vantage point of ease. We are frequently plagued with hard and difficult times, but it is out of these that we grow and mature and are able to view the future with expectancy. One particular author expressed this idea well although he wasn't writing from a Christian perspective: "It is only through struggling with the pain of our own crises, tragedies, sins, depressions, and problems that our greatness as human beings is realized. Our crises are anvils on which our growth is forged."[6]

But as our growth is forged on the anvil of experience, we can discover our capacity to dream and to use our imaginations creatively to the enrichment of our own lives and to the delight of others. Our imaginations deal with the *might-be* element in our lives.

So many of us, though, have allowed the so-called realities of life to so sterilize our minds and emotions that we've forgotten how to dream dreams and see visions—to draw on the richness of the world of make-believe. Referring back to the story of the little eagle who was raised as a chicken—our minds and God-given imaginations are meant to soar like an eagle, not to be used to peck around for corn in the dirt and muss of the chicken yard.

Enriching Imagination

One of the most delightful stories that pictures the richness that can be ours if we exercise our imaginations during our home-stretch years is told by Dr. Wayne Oates. Dr. Oates is a prominent counselor, psychologist, and professor in a graduate school of medicine. But he possesses the marvelous gift of a vivid and creative mind and imagination, even though he, too, is in the home stretch.

He writes,

> I was playing with our four-year-old grandson, Will, the other day. He loves to use our king-size bed as a trampoline. This time his feet were dirty, and I asked him to let me first wash his feet. Then he could jump on the bed.
>
> I took a warm and wet washcloth and washed his feet. Then I took the cloth to the bathroom to wash the dirt out of it. When I returned, Will was gone. I assumed he had gone out of the bedroom. Hence, I went about hanging a suit up and placing some shoes in the closet.
>
> Suddenly he jumped from behind the bed where he had been hiding. I reacted with great surprise, saying: "Where on earth did you come from, and how did you get in this room?" He said: "I came through that wall right there!" I said: "Well, I don't see any hole in the wall." He said: "I know. I fixed it back just like it was and painted it this color," pointing to a special color in the wallpaper. "And," he said, "if you will touch it with your finger, you will see that it's still wet paint." I reached and touched it with my finger and looked at my finger and said: "My goodness! You're right! It *is* still wet!" At which point both of us broke into hilarious laughter together. What fun! What magic![7]

Yes, that is a warm little story about a man and his grandson. But the point is that neither the grandfather nor his grandson will ever lose the warmth and richness of those magic moments, and both will be better people for having lived them. For both, the process of growth is wonderfully enhanced by their ability to think imaginatively and to dream.

The Drama of Optimism

There's another attractive quality of life that seems peculiar to "people on the grow"—they are alive with optimistic energy. In fact, I believe that growth and an openness to change can only be experienced by a person who is an optimist at heart.

To see the bright side of life, to look to the future with confidence and hope, is not to deny the difficult and rough times. Rather, it is to expect the best possible outcome or to dwell on the most hopeful aspects of any situation. And for the Christian, this definition is intimately a reality in Jesus Christ.

The drama of changing and growing as a person is nurtured by optimism and hope. Author Henri Nouwen has said, "An important part of the spiritual life is to keep longing, waiting, hoping, expecting."[8] This kind of a spirit is not for sissies as we wrestle with the growing process in the midlife and home-stretch years. Life is an ongoing journey of becoming.

It is the joyful and optimistic Christian who is alive to the opportunities for personal growth and is able to cope with the strains of life. And it is the Christian who has learned to dream and be imaginative and have an expectant and hopeful view of the future who, with God's help, can handle Evelyn Underhill's definition of what it means to be spiritually mature and alive:

> To be spiritually alive means to be growing and changing; not to settle down among a series of systemized beliefs and duties, but to endure and go on enduring the strains, conflicts and difficulties incident to development.
>
> Even the greatest spiritual teachers such as St. Paul and St. Augustine could never afford to relax the tension of their own spiritual lives; they never seem to stand still, are never afraid of conflict and change.[9]

The Christian on the Move

Picking up on what Evelyn Underhill has said, I would add that the growing Christian does not stand still; there is no relaxing. God doesn't intend for us to settle down and take it easy in any one place. This idea is wonderfully illustrated many places in the Bible, but two stories particularly stand out in my mind.

First, there's the story of Peter, James, and John, who had the awesome experience of being with Jesus on the mountaintop when he was transfigured. While Jesus was praying, "the aspect of his face was changed and his clothing became brilliant as lightning" (Luke 9:29, JB). Next, the three disciples saw Moses and Elijah with Jesus and overheard their conversation. This was a once-in-a-lifetime experience, and Peter immediately wanted to memorialize the event by building three monuments to mark the spot. But that was not to be; in a few moments, the scene had changed and Jesus was alone.

It wasn't lasting memorials that God wanted, but healed and changed lives. We shouldn't be too critical of Peter, though, because so often we face a similar temptation. We want to memorialize our spiritual high points and then go back to them again and again. But instead, as the disciples of Jesus learned, we are to be on the move—to grow and press ahead for new experiences.

Then there is the wonderful Old Testament story of the Tabernacle—God's first "dwelling place" within Israel. After the Hebrews had gotten settled in Canaan, there were those who felt that the portable tabernacle should be replaced by a permanent building—a temple like those stately buildings that their neighbors had constructed to the pagan gods. But it was too soon for such a structure. Israel's God was active and on the move. He was not to be restricted to one spot. In his plan, this was not a time for memorials.

It wasn't until much later that God allowed a temple to be built that would serve as his "dwelling place" among the people. But even that majestic temple did not last forever; it was leveled first by the armies of Babylon and then by those of Rome. The God of Israel and our God can never be confined to buildings, for he is a God of movement, of change, of growth.

An Example of Growth and Maturity

While the facts are sketchy, the story of John Mark in the New Testament seems to be a wonderful illustration of the transformation that can take place as a person grows in the Christian faith.

We first meet John Mark in the Garden of Gethsemane at the time of Jesus' arrest. It is likely he was about fifteen or sixteen at the time. We don't know how or why Mark was there or why he was apparently wearing nothing more than a sheet wrapped around him. But we do know that there was some kind of a scuffle, and a temple guard evidently tried to hold him. But Mark slipped out of the sheet and escaped naked from the garden.

Mark next appears some fifteen years later as he starts out with his uncle Barnabas and Paul on their first missionary journey. Evidently, he gave a good account of himself as they traveled through Cyprus. But when Paul and Barnabas and Mark landed on the south coast of Asia Minor and the decision was made to proceed north to Antioch of Pisidia, a Roman stronghold, Mark decided to desert his companions. We don't know the reason for his defection, but it is possible that his lack of maturity prompted him to leave rather than undergo the rigors of overland travel (or possibly he feared Roman persecution).

Paul and Barnabas went on alone, and while there was no rift in their relationship at that time, a break came later when Barnabas wanted to take Mark along on their second trip. Paul made it clear then that there was no place in his party for a quitter. His feelings were so strong that Paul and Barnabas separated and went different ways.

After that rather sad scene, Mark's life and activities are clothed in silence, and we have no idea what happened to him during those years. But we can conclude from two later references that he grew and matured as a man and in his Christian faith. After being rejected as a quitter by Paul at the beginning of the second missionary journey, he is next praised by the great apostle as being "profitable to me for the ministry" (2 Tim. 4:11). He is again mentioned by Paul in his letter to Philemon. And, of course, Mark's pilgrimage from immaturity to maturity is wonderfully apparent in the Gospel he wrote that bears his name.

The Prime Reason for Growth

We have stressed the importance of change and growth for the enrichment of our lives throughout every turn and straightaway and especially in the home stretch. But as Christians, our eyes are always on the future. Somehow I have to believe that our life here is a preparation for the future. In his incomparable style, C. S. Lewis gives us something serious to think about:

> Christianity asserts that every individual human being is going to live forever. . . . Now there are a good many things which would not be worth bothering about if I were going to live only seventy years, but which I had better bother about very seriously if I am going to live forever.[10]

Among those things worth bothering about, I believe, is an openness to change and a determination to grow in every way as we race down every yard of the home stretch.

Steps to a Rich and Rewarding Life

One of my dreams for many years has been to write a book on the home-stretch years of life. And for me, this is one of the most important chapters in the book. As I've worked through my thinking and feelings, especially in this chapter, certain very important ideas or steps to a rewarding life stand out in my mind. And as my own growth process continues with each new day, I think it will be helpful to be reminded of these high points that can and will move us on toward maturity as persons. I'm convinced that "to think on these things" can add years and zest to our lives:

Creative Disciples of Change and Growth

• *We are to avoid a "rocking chair" attitude as we move into the midlife and home-stretch years.* Joy in living and life-enriching experiences come from "living on the move."

• *If we don't change, we don't grow—and if we don't grow, we stagnate.* An eager openness to change keeps life exciting.

• *Doing new and unfamiliar things not only adds adventure to our lives, but also makes us interesting people to be with.*

• *We are never to be "too old to dream."* Dreaming dreams, seeing visions, using our God-given imaginations are keys that unlock our doors to the future.

• *To grow is to tackle each new day with optimism.* No one is ever made better by a pessimistic view of life. For the Christian, pessimism is a lack of faith; optimism sees God at work today and tomorrow.

• *The adventure of the future is always with us* as we plan and look ahead expectantly. The past is important only as it prepares us for the future.

The growing person doesn't live in a house with mirrors for walls, but in one with huge windows on every outside wall! It is not when we concentrate on reflections of ourselves, but when we look out into God's wonderful world and into the future, that satisfaction and fulfillment flood our lives and make us effective witnesses for the Lord.

Quality of Life
for the
Home Stretch

Our concern is for the quality of life rather than the quantity. And for those of us pragmatic and achievement-oriented citizens of this late twentieth-century Western world, this is sorely needed advice. Often we "run our race" with our eyes so glued to the track immediately in front of our feet that all we see is our own particular yard of dirt. We concentrate so heavily on ourselves— our successes, our needs and wants, our satisfaction— that we lose sight of everything else, including the richness of life and relationships that God wants us to have.

An unknown friar, probably writing in the home stretch of his life, is credited with this profound bit of reflection:

If I had my life to live over, I'd try to make more mistakes next time. I would relax, I would limber up; I would be sillier than I have been on this trip. I know of very few things I would take seriously. I would be less hygienic. I would take more chances. I would take more trips. I would climb more mountains, swim more rivers and watch more sunsets. I would eat more ice cream. I would have more actual troubles and fewer imaginary ones.

You see, I am one of those people who lives prophylactically and sensibly and sanely, hour after hour, day after day. Oh, I have had my moments and, if I had it to do over again, I'd have more of them. In fact, I'd try to have nothing else. Just moments, one after another, instead of living so many years ahead each day.

I've been one of those people who never go anywhere without a thermometer, a hot water bottle, a gargle, a raincoat, and a parachute. If I had it to do over again, I would go places and do things and travel lighter than I have.

If I had my life to live over again, I would start barefooted earlier in the spring and stay that way later in the fall. I would play hooky more; I wouldn't make such good grades except by accident. I would ride on more merry-go-rounds. I would pick more daisies!

I'm just very sure that wise and reflective friar had no intention for this to be taken as a literal autobiographical statement. Instead, I feel quite certain he was writing in parable form in order to express an enormously important truth.

Quality versus Quantity

He is wanting us, I believe, to be more concerned with the quality of life rather than the quantity. And for those of us pragmatic and achievement-oriented citizens of this late twentieth-century Western world, this is sorely needed advice. Often we "run our race" with our eyes so glued to the track immediately in front of our feet so that all we see is our own particular yard of dirt. We concentrate so heavily on ourselves—our successes, our needs and wants, and our satisfaction—that we lose sight of everything else, including the richness of life and relationships that God wants us to have.

With a somewhat different kind of expression, another unknown writer caught the sense of what I think the friar was trying to say with these words:

> For yesterday is but a dream,
> And tomorrow is only a vision;
> But today well lived makes every
>   yesterday a dream of happiness,
> And every tomorrow
>   a vision of hope.

Today well lived—this is what counts. It is the quality of life at each straightaway and turn that determines the quality at each future stage.

A Modern Example

One of the great present-day examples of the quality of life and a vision of hope is Claude Pepper, for many years a United States senator from Florida and now a member of the House of Representatives. At eighty-five, Claude Pepper is a dynamo in the United States Congress; he possesses a unique sense of humor. In an Associated Press release, the reporter wrote, "Despite two hearing aids, triple-focus glasses, a pacemaker in his chest, and two plastic valves in his heart, Pepper says he enjoys the daily challenges he encounters as chairman of the House Rules Committee and subcommittee chairman of the House Select Committee on Aging."

And then the reporter quoted Mr. Pepper directly: "I can't run ten miles in the afternoon, like I did in college, but I have a good car to take me there."[1]

Mr. Pepper's todays are "well lived" and his every tomorrow is obviously "a vision of hope." He has been heard to comment that he would be dead today if he had been forced to retire at sixty-five. He was not a victim of the idea that a person is a leftover at the age of sixty-five. Instead of slowing down as he moved into the home stretch, his pace picked up and the quality of his life became even richer as he pursued causes that he believes in with a passionate zeal. People like Mr. Pepper are *needed* and will be long remembered and revered for their energetic contribution to the welfare of others.

A Tragic Contrast

In vivid contrast to the relaxed and reflective friar and the dynamic Claude Pepper is the tragic story of an intense Old Testament king of Judah by the

name of Jehoram. Unlike his father, King
Jehoshaphat—who did "that which was right in the
sight of the Lord" (2 Chron. 20:32)—Jehoram was
a real rascal. When he became king on the death
of his father, he was thirty-two years old and
obviously very insecure—in addition to having a
perverted sense of what was right and wrong. One
of his first acts after being crowned king was to kill
off all possible opposition, including members of his
own family.

Jehoram's eight-year reign was a succession of one
evil act after another—it was a black time in Judah's
history. But at the age of forty, he died an agonizing
death from a loathsome and incurable disease that
had plagued him for two years. The writer of 2
Chronicles 21:19–20 says, "His people made no
burning for him"—(there was no time of mourning)
and he "departed without being desired" (he was
no longer wanted or needed; they were glad to see
him die). The quality of Jehoram's life was such that
he left nothing good behind him and nobody missed
him or was sorry that he was gone. This has to be
the ultimate tragedy!

One of our deepest longings in life is to feel needed
and wanted—to feel that someone cares, that we
have worth to them. But in contrast to Jehoram's
self-centered and evil lifestyle, feelings of worth come
from having a full and rich life—the kind Jesus
promised (John 10:10) and wants us to enjoy. And
all of this becomes possible, I believe, by practicing

a lifestyle symbolized in the reflections of the friar quoted at the beginning of this chapter.

A Healthy Perspective

A quality of life that can make a positive difference is epitomized not by the traveler who always takes "a thermometer, a hot water bottle, a gargle, a raincoat, and a parachute" when he travels, but by one who wants to "ride on more merry-go-rounds." This is a person with a healthy perspective, a sense of humor—one who doesn't take himself too seriously. It is as "we pick more daisies" that we are open to the fullness of God and the exuberant joy he wants us to have.

Now, don't misunderstand me. We *are* to take God seriously. But this doesn't mean living as if the weight of the world was on *our* shoulders, as if God's mission in the world depended *only* on us and our sobriety. So often, instead of clustering joyfully with people in search of God, we draw apart with pained expressions on our faces and talk with a somber tone and inflection in language that is foreign to any except those who are a part of our particular "in group."

In his book entitled *The Humor of Christ,* Dr. Elton Trueblood quotes from an old pamphlet, entitled *God in Everything,* published by Epworth Press. Parson John is writing to Miriam Gray and says,

> Many of the religious people that I know, when they
> talk of religion, have a bedside manner and walk

110

about in felt slippers. And if they speak of God they always tidy themselves first. But *you* go in and out of all the rooms in God's house as though you were quite at home. You open the doors without knocking and you hum on the stairs, and it isn't always hymns either. My aunt thinks you are not quite reverent; but then, she can keep felt slippers on her mind without any trouble.

Dr. Trueblood then goes on to stress the fact that the Christian is to be full of joy, even in the midst of difficult circumstances, because he or she knows that God's purposes will ultimately be accomplished.[2]

It seems to me that a quality of life that enriches our midlife and home-stretch years and in turn helps us to make life better for others is a healthy sense of humor that helps us to keep ourselves in a proper perspective. It is fun to be around a person who enjoys life and can see its humorous side as well as its serious one. In fact, I believe it is this kind of person who witnesses most effectively to the goodness and greatness of God. People don't find Christ in buildings, but in other people—attractive and winsome people who enjoy themselves and others.

I like the kind of humor and sense of purpose expressed by a Catholic sister I read about somewhere: "We can't sit here forever and listen to our arteries harden. We have to get out of our little nunny world." Or, picking up on Parson John's comments as quoted by Elton Trueblood—we've got to get the felt slippers off of our minds and be about the joy of living in a big world. As Bishop Fulton Sheen once said, "The amount of humor that anyone gets out of the world is the size of the world in which he lives." And God has set us down in a *big* world.

Accentuate the Positives

Throughout all of life, but especially at midlife and then on into the home stretch, our lives are meant to be full of good humor, of the fullness of joy— we are to "make a joyful noise unto the Lord" (Ps. 98:4). But so often the quality of our lives suffers because we concentrate on the negatives. Joy Davidman opens her readable and provocative book, *Smoke on the Mountain,* with this thought-provoking story:

There is a tale told of a missionary in a dark corner of Africa where the men had a habit of filing their teeth to sharp points. He was hard at work trying to convert a native chief. Now, the chief was very old, and the missionary was very Old Testament— his version of Christianity leaned heavily on thou-shalt-not's. The savage listened patiently.

"I do not understand," he said at last. "You tell me that I must not take my neighbor's wife."

"That's right," said the missionary.

112

Quality of Life for the Home Stretch

"Or his ivory, or his oxen."

"Quite right."

"And I must not dance the war dance and then ambush him on the trail and kill him."

"Absolutely right!"

"But I cannot do any of these things!" said the savage regretfully. "I am too old. To be old and to be Christian, they are the same thing!"[3]

Our danger as Christians in the home stretch is that so often we act "old." We lose sight, as this missionary evidently had, of the truth that the God of the Old Testament is also the God of the New—that he was and is a God of love as well as justice. As a matter of fact, the "first and great commandment" of Jesus in Matthew 22 is a quotation from both Deuteronomy and Leviticus in the Old Testament.

Contrast the message the African chief got from the missionary and his understanding of it with the attitude of writer Booth Tarkington. When he was seventy-five years old, someone asked whether old people felt old in spirit. "I don't know," he answered. "Why don't you ask someone who is old?" Or with the controversial contemporary scientist Dr. Linus Pauling. We saw him interviewed on television while this chapter was being written. At eighty-five, he was full of life and optimism and held a confident view of the future. In fact, the reason for his appearance was to promote his new book entitled *How to Live Longer and Feel Better*.

113

Quality of Life for the Home Stretch

A Shared Faith

It is this quality of living that gives flavor and color and zest to life, that helps us feel wanted and needed, that gives us the resources to make a difference in the lives of others. Remember, for the Christian, eternal life in Christ is *now,* and it is meant to be rich and fulfilling.

One of the greatest joys of being a Christian comes as we share our faith with our families and those with whom we work and play and worship. But sharing our faith is more than a joy; it is what the Lord instructed us to do. I repeat: people don't meet and discover Christ in buildings but in other people, not in plays and concerts but in performers and actors. Christ isn't discovered merely in people with a Christian label but in "doers of the Word."

But our assignment as Christian witnesses isn't to carry sandwich boards emblazoned with warnings or proof texts. Rather, it is to act and live our faith in the joy of the Lord who makes a difference in each of our worlds.

A Present Pattern for an Exciting Future

"The straight part of a race track from the last turn to the finish"—the home stretch—calls for our greatest and most creative efforts. It will be IF . . .

114

Quality of Life for the Home Stretch

• *We strain ahead for what is still to come and see in each day an adventure of faith.* We have made the deliberate decision to choose life.

• *We don't approach life with a "sneeze mentality"—acting as if life were a series of reflex actions over which we have no control.* It is our attitudes that determine life's meaning and direction. And as Christians, we are to live energized by positive attitudes—we are not grasshoppers in a world of giants, but eagles designed by God to soar.

• *We live with exuberant enthusiasm.* Sam Goldwin, pioneer moviemaker, once said, "Enthusiasm for what you are doing is, I think, the key to success. I know that in picture-making you have to have enthusiasm, love, and affection and excitement about the picture you are making. . . . I have found enthusiasm for work and life to be the most precious ingredient in any recipe for successful living."[4]

This same kind of enthusiasm and optimism shines through in a comment sixty-two-year-old actor Charlton Heston made in a recent interview, "You know, I've been a very lucky man. I have no regrets. There are still lots of roles I want to play, much I want to do. And, inside, I still feel like a young man full of optimism and wonder."[5]

• *We give top priority in our lives to making friends and being a friend.* The writer of Ecclesiastes understood the importance of friendship when he wrote, "Two are better than one, because they have

115

a good reward for their labor. For if they fall, one will lift up his companion. But woe to him who is alone when he falls, for he has no one to help him up. . . . how can one be warm alone?" (4:9–11, NKJV).

Having a friend, being a friend—sometimes a mentor—means we're not alone. It is through friendship that our lives are enriched and our influence on others becomes effective.

• *We remember that growing and maturing in life and in the Christian faith comes from an awareness of being fully alive, an openness to change, and a willingness to dream.* A child asks, "Where did I come from?" A teenager asks, "What shall I do?" The mature person asks, "What shall I become?"

It is a little like looking into a kaleidoscope—when we hold it up to our eye, the beautiful pattern almost takes our breath away. But unless we turn it, we'll miss the beautiful design that comes with the change. This is what life is meant to be like for the growing Christian. As we change and mature, life becomes increasingly beautiful with each change.

To cling to the past, to hang on to the present is to miss the joy of the home stretch. With St. Paul, we forget the past and press on with the words of Jesus always before us, "For whosoever will save his life shall lose it; but whosoever shall lose his life for my sake and the gospel's, the same shall save it" (Mark 8:35).

Notes

Chapter 1

1. Viktor E. Frankl, *Man's Search for Meaning* (Boston: Beacon, 1959, 1962), 72.
2. Paul Tournier, *Learn to Grow Old* (Harper & Row, 1972), 12.
3. I have been unable to locate the source for this wonderful story. This omission will gladly be rectified in future printings when and if the source is located.

Chapter 2

1. Ben Campbell Johnson, *The Heart of Paul: 2 Corinthians 11:23–27* (Waco, TX: Word, 1976), 102.

Chapter 3

1. C. S. Lewis, *Mere Christianity* (New York: Macmillan/Collier, 1943, 1945, 1952), 117.
2. Bruce Larson, *My Creator, My Friend* (Waco, TX: Word, 1986), 191–192.
3. Arthur Gordon, *A Touch of Wonder* (Old Tappan, NJ: Revell, 1974), 143–148.

4. Cecil G. Osborne, *The Art of Becoming a Whole Person* (Waco, TX: Word, 1978), 85.

5. Ibid., 86.

Chapter 4

1. Paul Tournier, *To Understand Each Other* (Atlanta: John Knox, 1967), 8.

2. Floyd and Harriett Thatcher, *Long Term Marriage* (Waco, TX: Word, 1980), 83.

3. Henri Nouwen, *Out of Solitude* (Notre Dame, IN: Ave Maria, 1974).

4. The story appeared in *Creative Help for Daily Living* under the title, "The Gift of Friendship," © 1980, Foundation for Christian Living, Pawling, NY.

5. Ted W. Engstrom with Robert C. Larson, *The Fine Art of Friendship* (Nashville: Thomas Nelson, 1985), 13.

Chapter 5

1. Elizabeth Yates, *Call It Zest* (Brattleboro, VT: Stephen Greene, 1977), 22.

2. Joan Saunders Wixen, "Twentieth Century Miracle Maker," *Modern Maturity,* December 1984– January 1985, 96.

3. Gail Sheehy, *Passages* (New York: Dutton, 1976), 353.

4. Mildred Newman and Bernard Berkowitz with Jean Owen, *How to Be Your Own Best Friend* (New York: Random House, 1971), 19.

5. "Women Reveal Secrets of Longevity," Associated Press article in *Waco Tribune-Herald,* 27 May 1985.

6. Harold C. Lyons, Jr., *Tenderness Is Strength* (New York: Harper & Row, 1977), 23.

7. Wayne E. Oates, *The Struggle to Be Free* (Philadelphia: Westminster, 1983), 162–163.

8. Henri Nouwen, *The Genesee Diary* (New York: Doubleday, 1976).

9. Evelyn Underhill, *The House of the Soul and Concerning the Inner Life* (Minneapolis: Winston-Seabury, 1926, 1929).

10. C. S. Lewis, *Mere Christianity* (New York: Macmillan/Collier, 1943, 1945, 1952), 73.

Chapter 6

1. "85-Year-Old Denounces Retirement," Associated Press article in *Waco Tribune-Herald,* 13 March 1986.

2. Elton Trueblood, *The Humor of Christ* (New York: Harper & Row, 1964), 31–32.

3. Joy Davidman, *Smoke on the Mountain* (Philadelphia: Westminster, 1953, 1954), 13.

4. Sam Goldwin, "Creating with Enthusiasm," *Nation's Business,* November 1966.

5. Dotson Rader, "If I Ran and Won, I'd Never Be Able to Act Again," *Parade,* 9 March 1986.